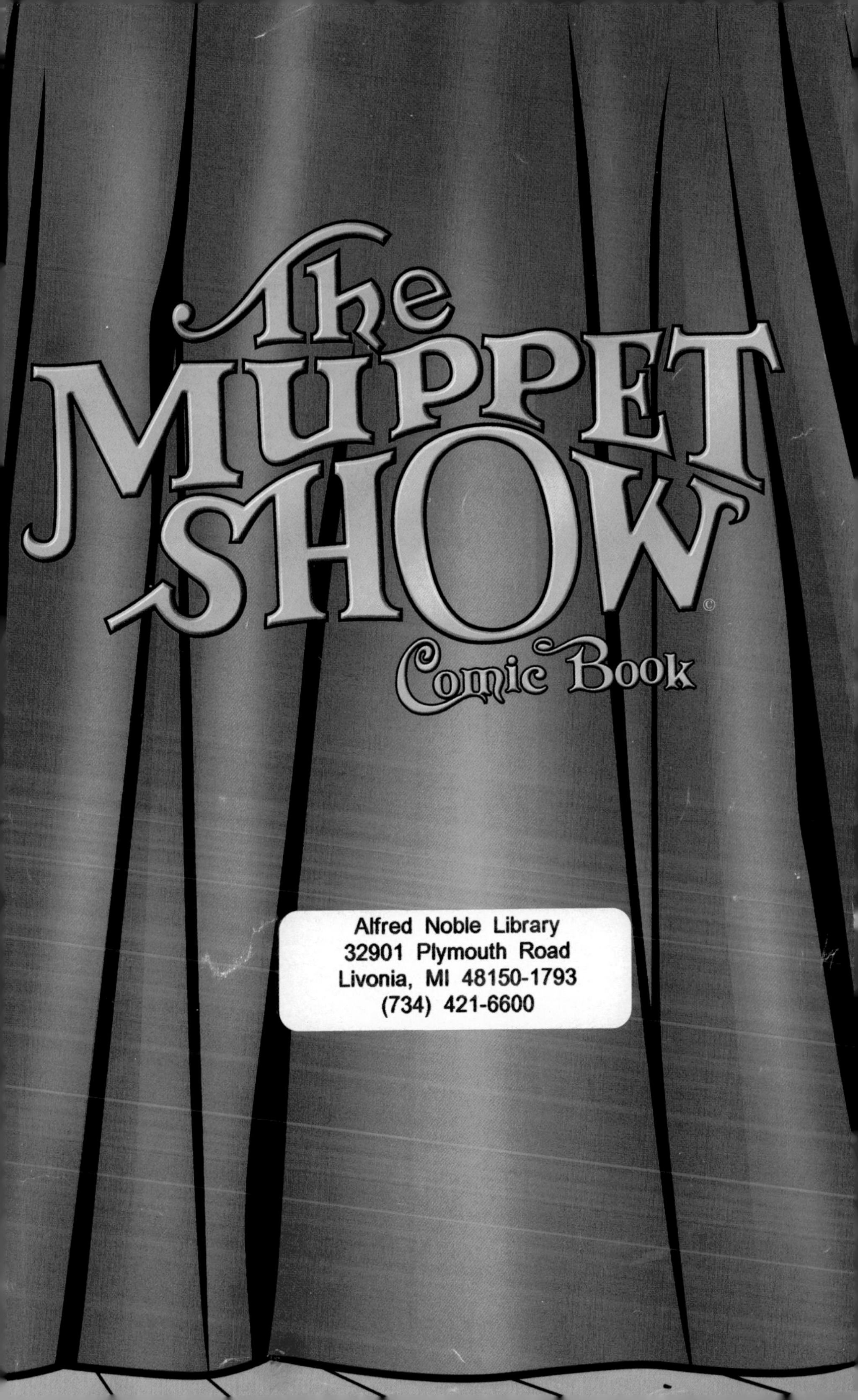
The
MUPPET
SHOW©
Comic Book

The MUPPET SHOW

Comic Book

SPECIAL THANKS: TISHANA
WILLIAMS, IVONNE FELICIANO,
AND THE MUPPETS STUDIO

AND A VERY HEARTY ROUND
OF APPLAUSE FOR DAVE
SHELTON!

THE MUPPET SHOW – July 2009 published by BOOM! KIDS, a division of Boom Entertainment, Inc. All conten
2009 The Muppets Studio, LLC. BOOM! KIDS and the BOOM! KIDS logo are trademarks of Boom Entertainm
Inc., registered in various countries and categories. All rights reserved. Office of publication: 6310 San Vice

Meet the Muppets

WRITTEN AND DRAWN BY	Roger Langridge
COLORS	Digikore Studios
LETTERS	Deron Bennett
EDITOR	Paul Morrissey
COVERS	Roger Langridge

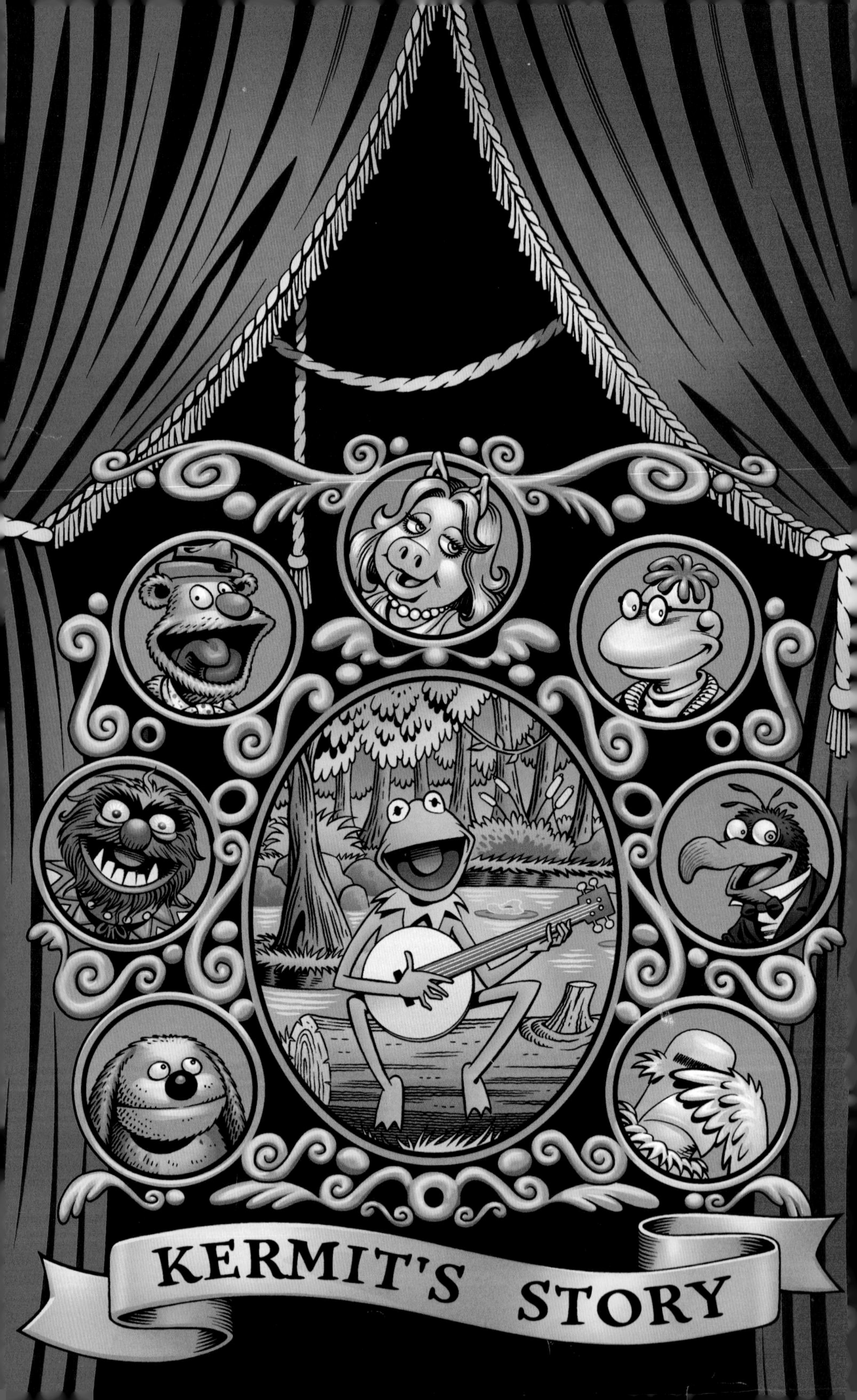
KERMIT'S STORY

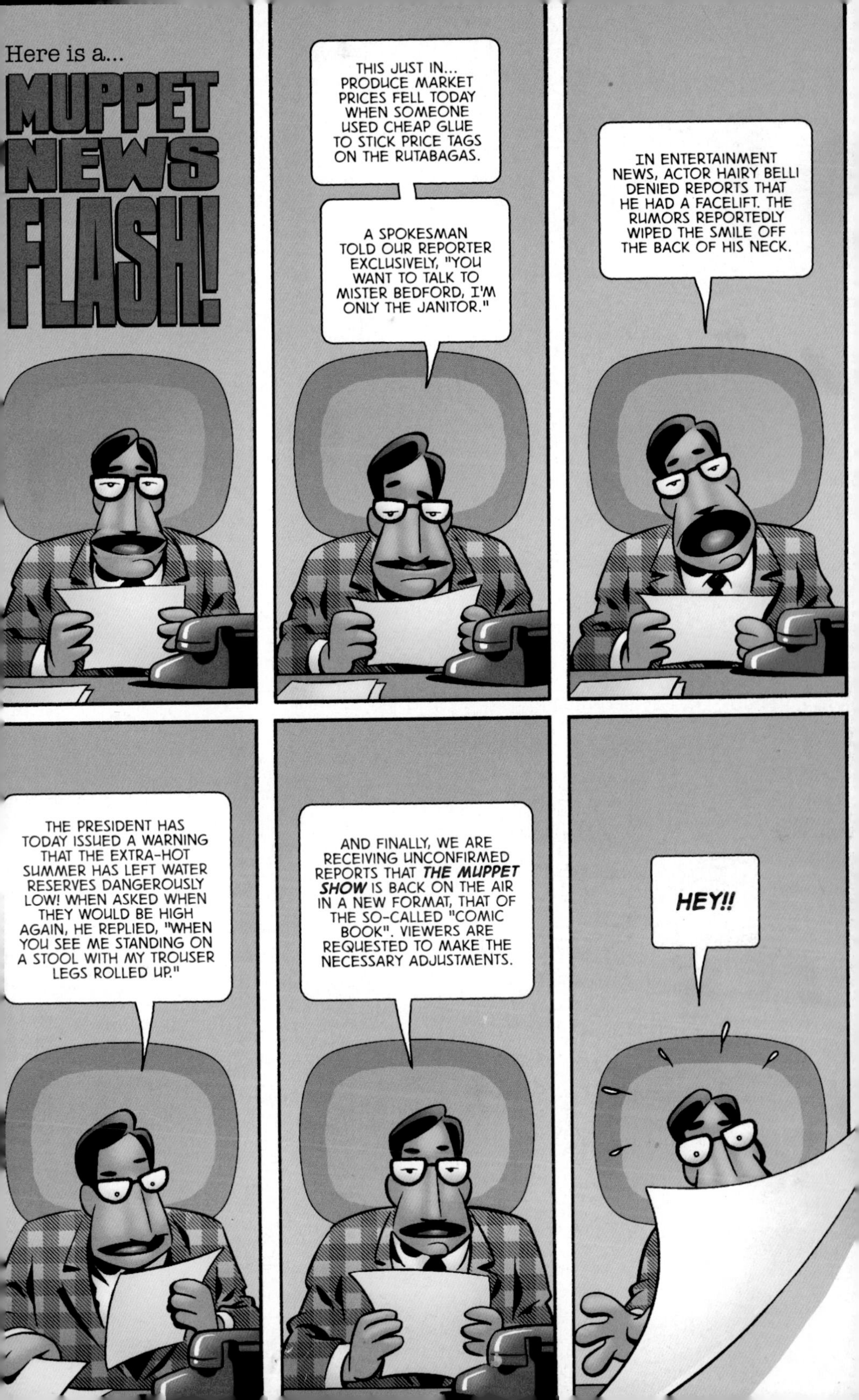
Here is a...
MUPPET NEWS FLASH!
THIS JUST IN... PRODUCE MARKET PRICES FELL TODAY WHEN SOMEONE USED CHEAP GLUE TO STICK PRICE TAGS ON THE RUTABAGAS.
A SPOKESMAN TOLD OUR REPORTER EXCLUSIVELY, "YOU WANT TO TALK TO MISTER BEDFORD, I'M ONLY THE JANITOR."
IN ENTERTAINMENT NEWS, ACTOR HAIRY BELLI DENIED REPORTS THAT HE HAD A FACELIFT. THE RUMORS REPORTEDLY WIPED THE SMILE OFF THE BACK OF HIS NECK.
THE PRESIDENT HAS TODAY ISSUED A WARNING THAT THE EXTRA-HOT SUMMER HAS LEFT WATER RESERVES DANGEROUSLY LOW! WHEN ASKED WHEN THEY WOULD BE HIGH AGAIN, HE REPLIED, "WHEN YOU SEE ME STANDING ON A STOOL WITH MY TROUSER LEGS ROLLED UP."
AND FINALLY, WE ARE RECEIVING UNCONFIRMED REPORTS THAT *THE MUPPET SHOW* IS BACK ON THE AIR IN A NEW FORMAT, THAT OF THE SO-CALLED "COMIC BOOK". VIEWERS ARE REQUESTED TO MAKE THE NECESSARY ADJUSTMENTS.
HEY!!

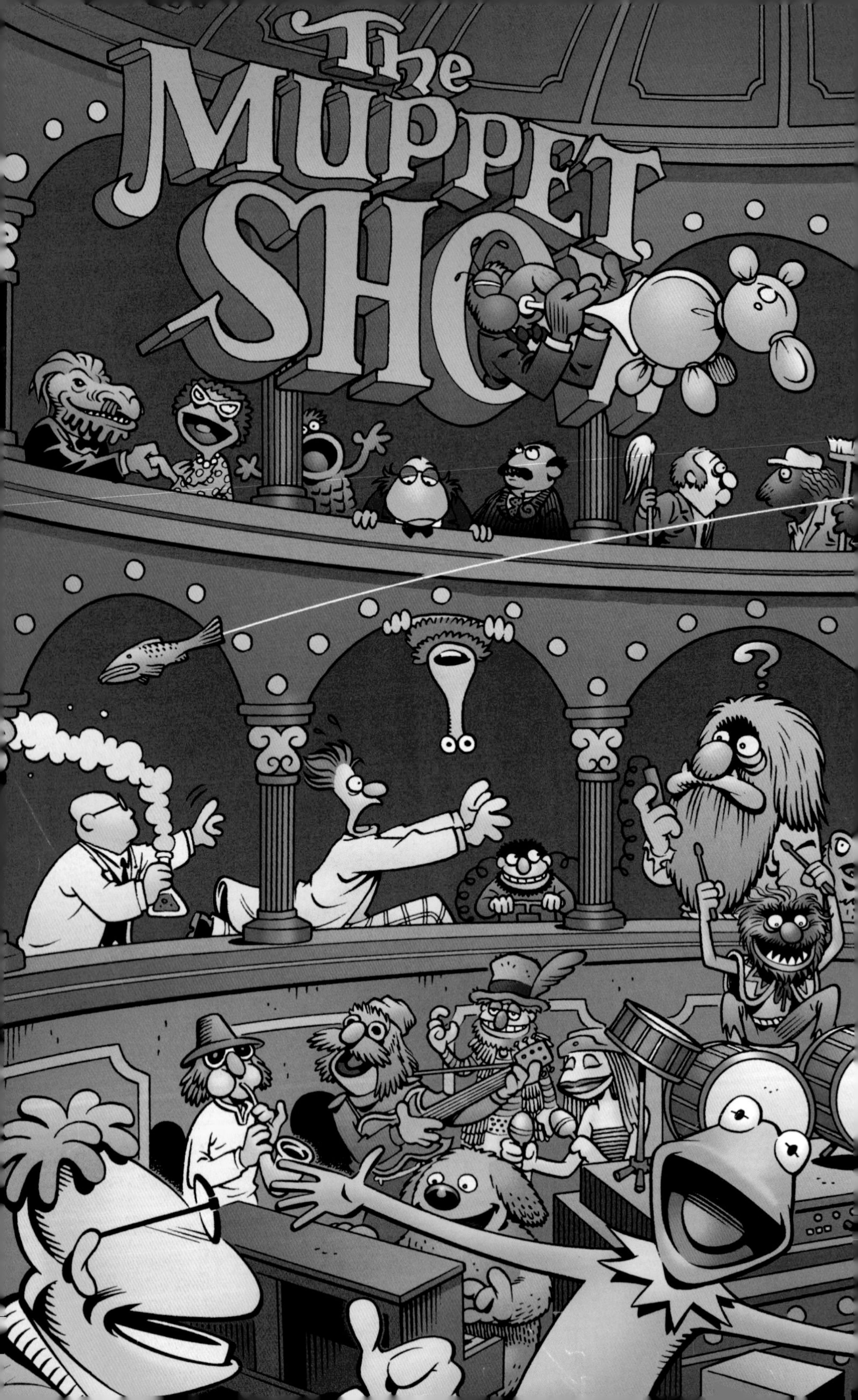
The
MUPPET
SHO

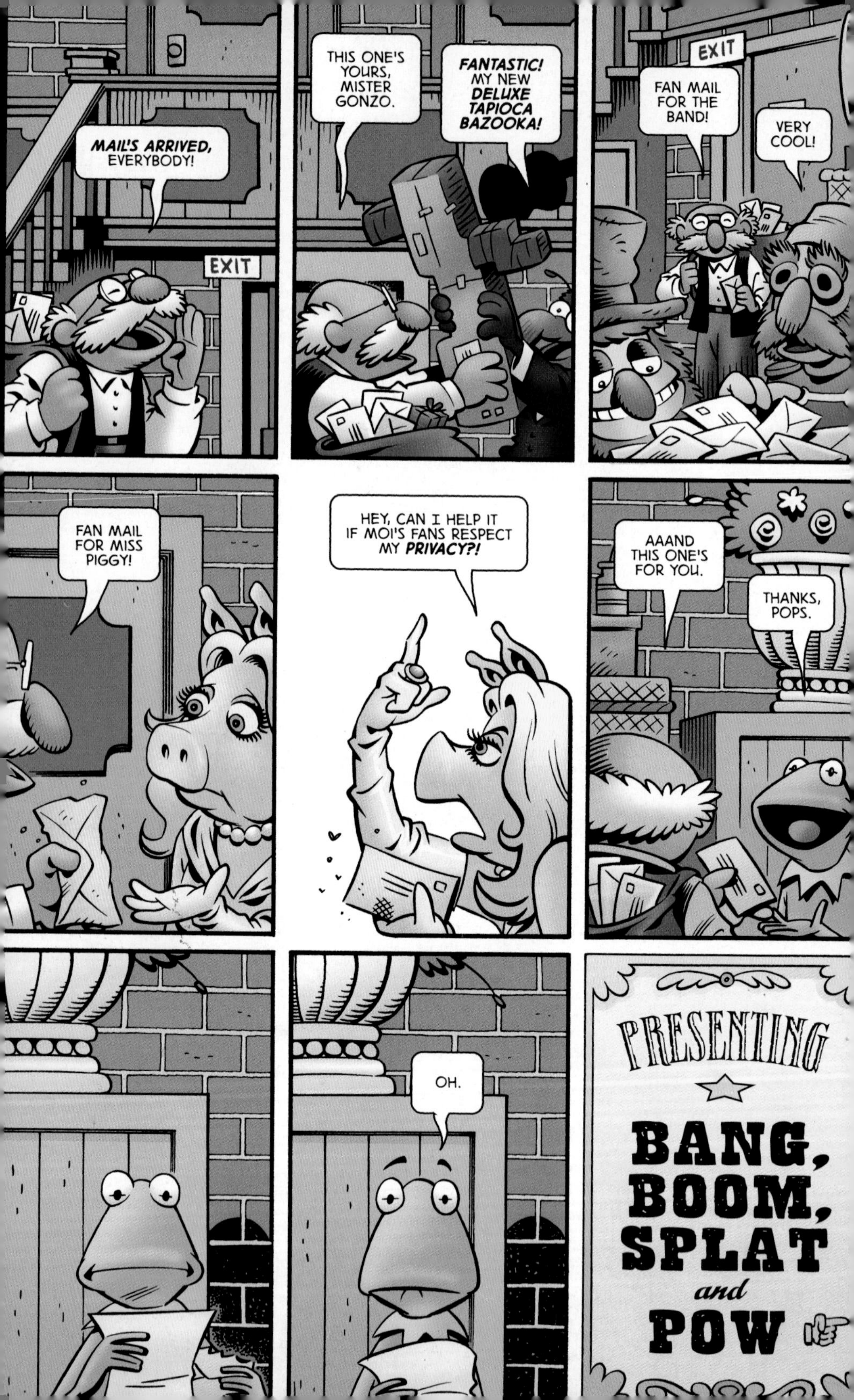
MAIL'S ARRIVED, EVERYBODY!
EXIT
THIS ONE'S YOURS, MISTER GONZO.
FANTASTIC! MY NEW DELUXE TAPIOCA BAZOOKA!
EXIT
FAN MAIL FOR THE BAND!
VERY COOL!
FAN MAIL FOR MISS PIGGY!
HEY, CAN I HELP IT IF MOI'S FANS RESPECT MY PRIVACY?!
AAAND THIS ONE'S FOR YOU.
THANKS, POPS.
OH.
PRESENTING
BANG, BOOM, SPLAT and POW

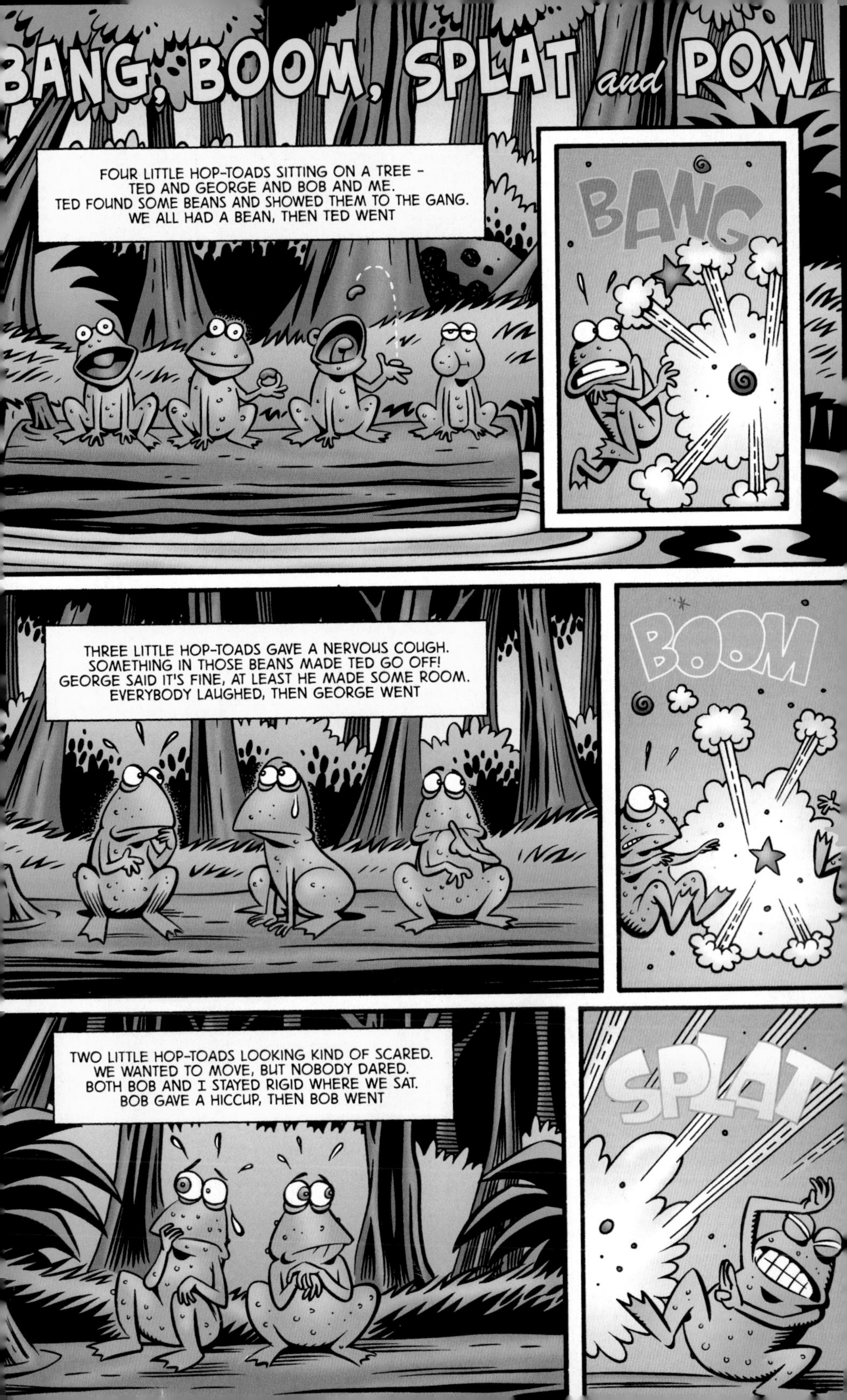
BANG, BOOM, SPLAT and POW
FOUR LITTLE HOP-TOADS SITTING ON A TREE – TED AND GEORGE AND BOB AND ME. TED FOUND SOME BEANS AND SHOWED THEM TO THE GANG. WE ALL HAD A BEAN, THEN TED WENT
BANG
THREE LITTLE HOP-TOADS GAVE A NERVOUS COUGH. SOMETHING IN THOSE BEANS MADE TED GO OFF! GEORGE SAID IT'S FINE, AT LEAST HE MADE SOME ROOM. EVERYBODY LAUGHED, THEN GEORGE WENT
BOOM
TWO LITTLE HOP-TOADS LOOKING KIND OF SCARED. WE WANTED TO MOVE, BUT NOBODY DARED. BOTH BOB AND I STAYED RIGID WHERE WE SAT. BOB GAVE A HICCUP, THEN BOB WENT
SPLAT

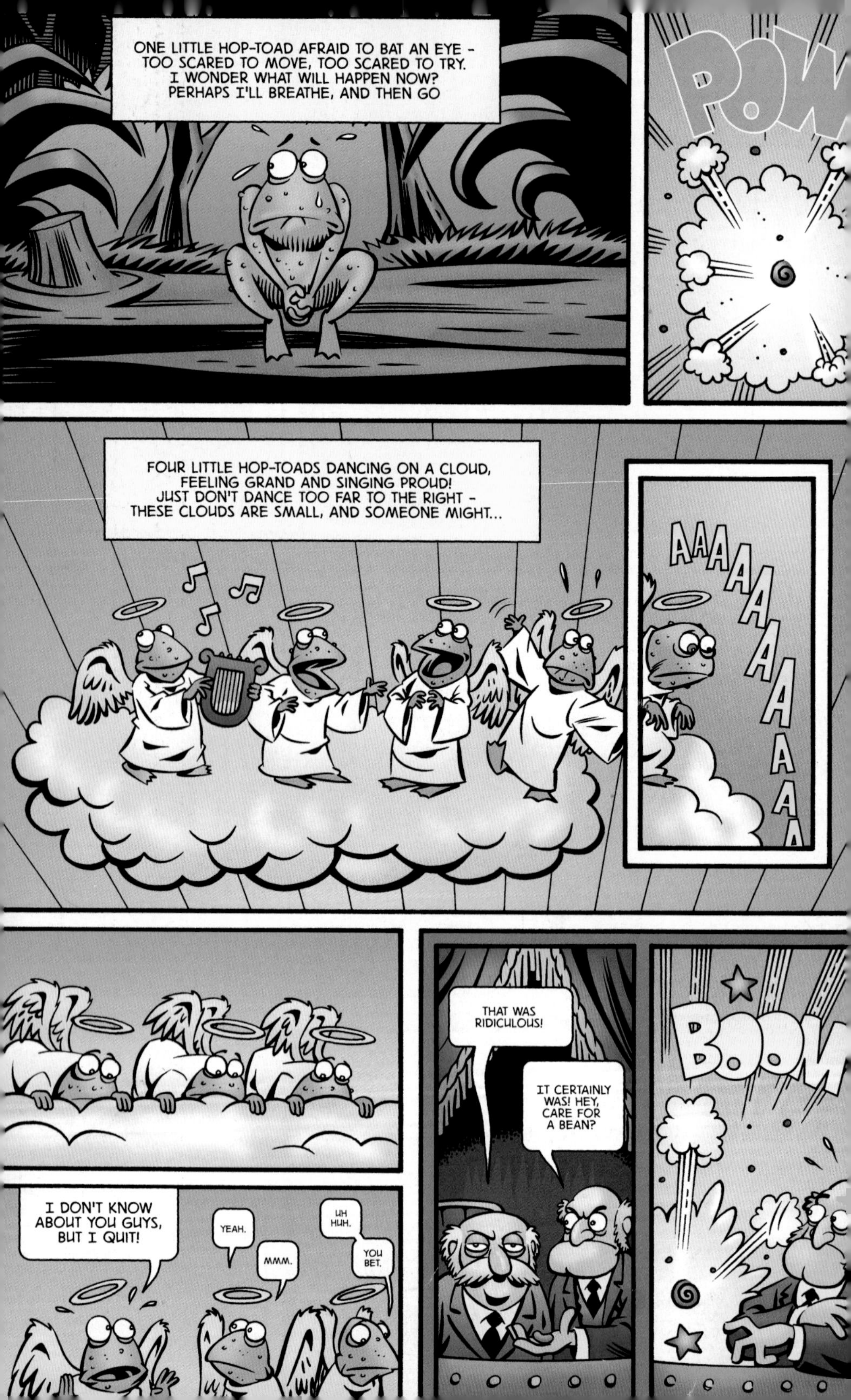
ONE LITTLE HOP-TOAD AFRAID TO BAT AN EYE - TOO SCARED TO MOVE, TOO SCARED TO TRY. I WONDER WHAT WILL HAPPEN NOW? PERHAPS I'LL BREATHE, AND THEN GO
POW
FOUR LITTLE HOP-TOADS DANCING ON A CLOUD, FEELING GRAND AND SINGING PROUD! JUST DON'T DANCE TOO FAR TO THE RIGHT - THESE CLOUDS ARE SMALL, AND SOMEONE MIGHT...
AAAAAAAAAAAA
I DON'T KNOW ABOUT YOU GUYS, BUT I QUIT!
YEAH.
MMM.
UH HUH.
YOU BET.
THAT WAS RIDICULOUS!
IT CERTAINLY WAS! HEY, CARE FOR A BEAN?
BOOM

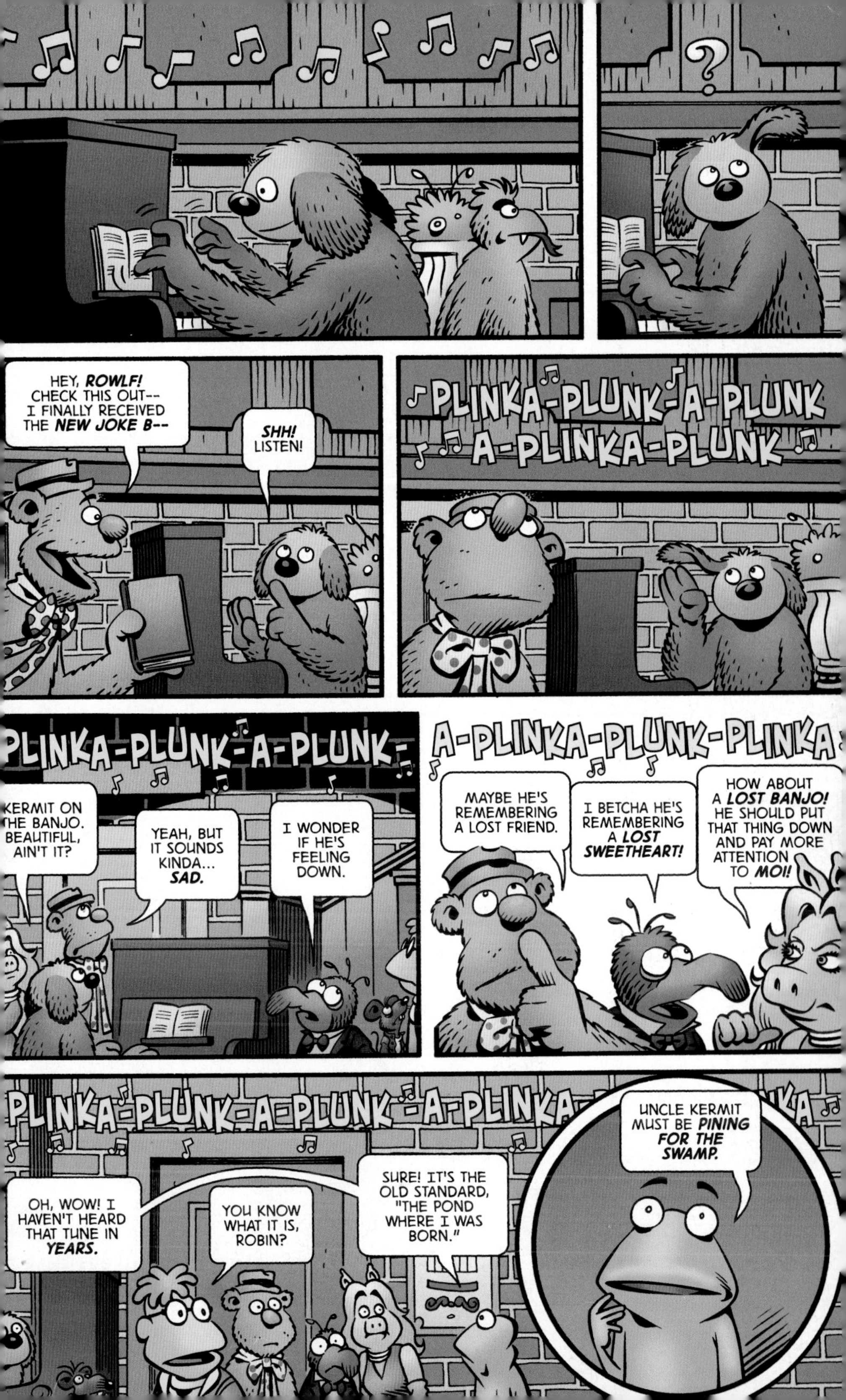
?
HEY, ROWLF! CHECK THIS OUT-- I FINALLY RECEIVED THE NEW JOKE B--
SHH! LISTEN!
PLINKA-PLUNK-A-PLUNK
A-PLINKA-PLUNK
PLINKA-PLUNK-A-PLUNK-
KERMIT ON THE BANJO. BEAUTIFUL, AIN'T IT?
YEAH, BUT IT SOUNDS KINDA... SAD.
I WONDER IF HE'S FEELING DOWN.
A-PLINKA-PLUNK-PLINKA
MAYBE HE'S REMEMBERING A LOST FRIEND.
I BETCHA HE'S REMEMBERING A LOST SWEETHEART!
HOW ABOUT A LOST BANJO! HE SHOULD PUT THAT THING DOWN AND PAY MORE ATTENTION TO MOI!
PLINKA-PLUNK-A-PLUNK-A-PLINKA-
OH, WOW! I HAVEN'T HEARD THAT TUNE IN YEARS.
YOU KNOW WHAT IT IS, ROBIN?
SURE! IT'S THE OLD STANDARD, "THE POND WHERE I WAS BORN."
UNCLE KERMIT MUST BE PINING FOR THE SWAMP.

CLOSE ENCOUNTERS of the WORST KIND

THE POOBS ARE A FAMOUSLY PEACEFUL RACE OF BEINGS, AND THE KOOZEBANIANS HAVE BEEN AWAITING THIS HISTORIC MEETING FOR GENERATIONS! AS YOU CAN SEE, THEY ARE VERY EXCITED ABOUT THE PROSPECT.

WELL, AH, YES. HERE WE ARE ON THE PLANET KOOZEBANE, AND IT'S A VERY EXCITING MOMENT, BECAUSE WE ARE ABOUT TO WITNESS THE FIRST CONTACT BETWEEN THE NATIVE KOOZEBANIANS AND THEIR CLOSEST GALACTIC NEIGHBORS, THE POOBS.

APPARENTLY, KOOZEBANE ORIGINALLY MADE CONTACT WITH THE POOBS BY INTERCEPTING THEIR RADIO BROADCASTS! EACH RADIO WAVE HAS TAKEN ELEVEN YEARS TO REACH HERE, AND EACH REPLY HAS TAKEN ANOTHER ELEVEN YEARS TO RETURN TO THE PLANET POOBATRON.

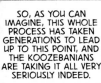

SO, AS YOU CAN IMAGINE, THIS WHOLE PROCESS HAS TAKEN GENERATIONS TO LEAD UP TO THIS POINT, AND THE KOOZEBANIANS ARE TAKING IT ALL VERY SERIOUSLY INDEED.

AND NOW IT LOOKS AS IF THE POOB SHIP IS COMING IN TO LAND! THIS IS INCREDIBLE, LADIES AND GENTLEMEN-- WE ARE WITNESSING THE FIRST MEETING BETWEEN TWO ALIEN RACES! WHAT AN ASTONISHING SYMBOL OF THE DESIRE FOR PEACEFUL CONTACT BETWEEN THEIR CULTURES!

SPLAT

ER, AH... WELL, HERE ON KOOZEBANE THINGS AREN'T QUITE WORKING OUT AS WE'D HOPED. JOIN ME HERE AGAIN SOON, WHERE I'LL ALMOST CERTAINLY BE ACTING AS OFFICIAL WAR CORRESPONDENT.

IN ABOUT A WEEK, BY THE LOOK OF THINGS.

ARE WE ON?

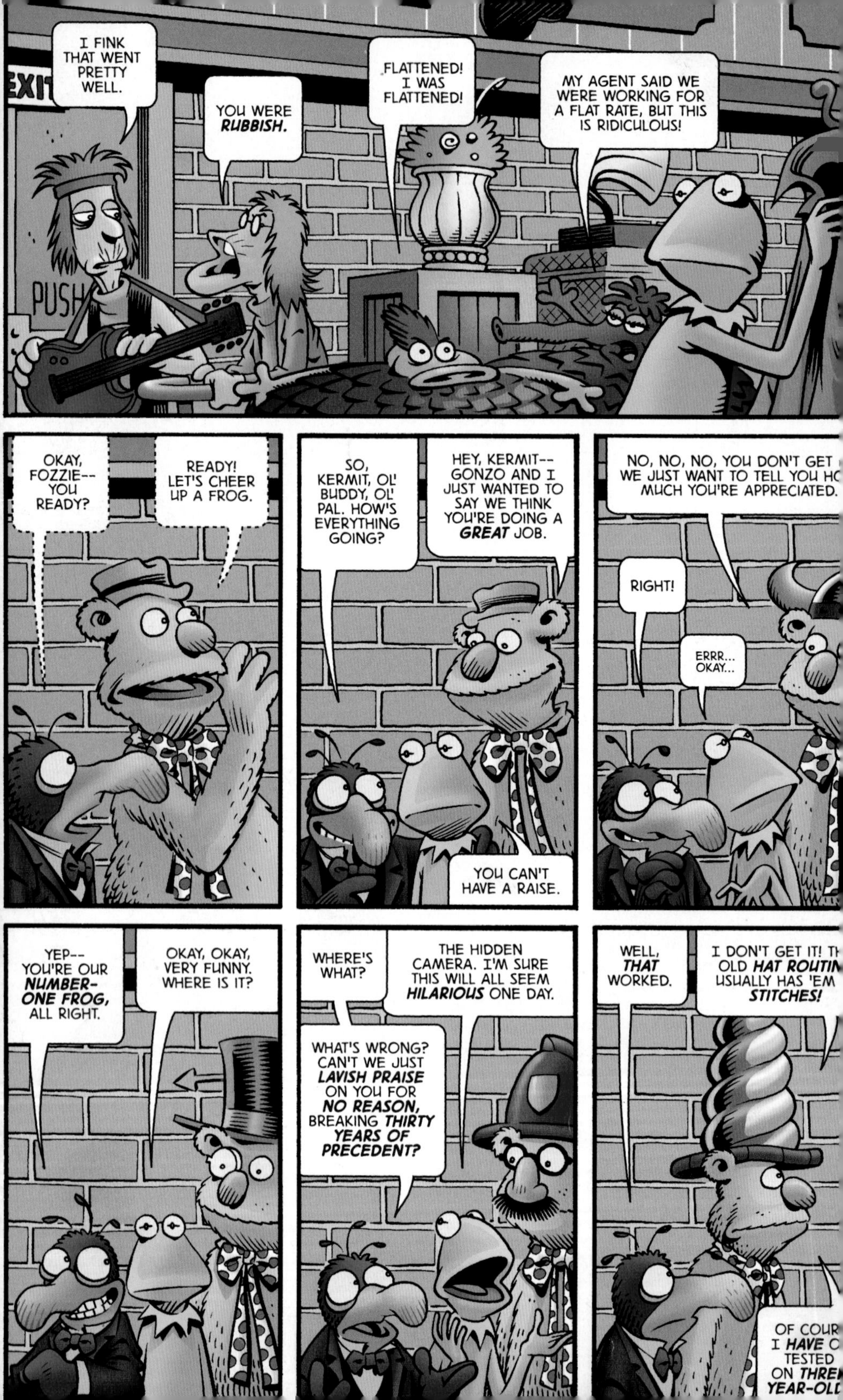

EXIT
PUSH
I FINK THAT WENT PRETTY WELL.
YOU WERE **RUBBISH.**
FLATTENED! I WAS FLATTENED!
MY AGENT SAID WE WERE WORKING FOR A FLAT RATE, BUT THIS IS RIDICULOUS!
OKAY, FOZZIE-- YOU READY?
READY! LET'S CHEER UP A FROG.
SO, KERMIT, OL' BUDDY, OL' PAL. HOW'S EVERYTHING GOING?
HEY, KERMIT-- GONZO AND I JUST WANTED TO SAY WE THINK YOU'RE DOING A **GREAT** JOB.
YOU CAN'T HAVE A RAISE.
NO, NO, NO, YOU DON'T GET
WE JUST WANT TO TELL YOU H
MUCH YOU'RE APPRECIATED.
RIGHT!
ERRR... OKAY...
YEP-- YOU'RE OUR ***NUMBER-ONE FROG,*** ALL RIGHT.
OKAY, OKAY, VERY FUNNY. WHERE IS IT?
WHERE'S WHAT?
THE HIDDEN CAMERA. I'M SURE THIS WILL ALL SEEM ***HILARIOUS*** ONE DAY.
WHAT'S WRONG? CAN'T WE JUST ***LAVISH PRAISE*** ON YOU FOR ***NO REASON,*** BREAKING ***THIRTY YEARS OF PRECEDENT?***
WELL, ***THAT*** WORKED.
I DON'T GET IT! T
OLD ***HAT ROUTI***
USUALLY HAS 'EM
STITCHES!
OF COU
I ***HAVE***
TESTED
ON ***THRE***
YEAR-OL

GENIUS! WHEN UNCLE KERMIT TASTES THIS *LILY PAD GOULASH,* HE'LL EITHER BE *DELIGHTED* OR HE'LL REMEMBER WHY HE LEFT THE SWAMP IN THE *FIRST* PLACE!

EITHER WAY, WE'RE *GOLDEN!*

1001 SWAMP RECIPES

CHEF! I NEED YOUR HELP! CAN I ASK YOU TO *WHIP SOMETHING UP...?*

HØER BORSCHT DER *FÄER* DER BÖERKEN...

SEE THIS RECIPE? I NEED YOU TO PREPARE IT FOR UNCLE KERMIT.

VANTER MOE DER *CØEKER DER PÄEPER?*

NO, NO, NO... LET'S SEE, HOW CAN I MAKE THIS CLEARER?... ME WANT YOU TO COOK DISH FOR FROG! *DISH FOR FROG!* SEE?

DOEMT VIT HÖERBE KERMT *GÄSSE MØURK SCHIX?*

GAS MARK SIX! OKAY, I THINK WE'RE GETTING SOMEWHERE. *GOULASH FOR FROGS AT GAS MARK SIX!*

JÄ, JÄ! *CØEKER DER FRÖEGGY-FRÖEGGY ŒURF DER GÄSSE MØURK SCHIX!*

CØEKER DER FRÖEGGY-FRÖEGGY!

AAGH! NO, *WAIT,* YOU'RE MAKING A *TERRIBLE--*

CØEKER DER FRÖEGGY-FRÖEGGY ŒURF DER *GÄSSE MØURK SCHIX!* JÄ, JÄ!

AND NOW ...

The Swedish Chef

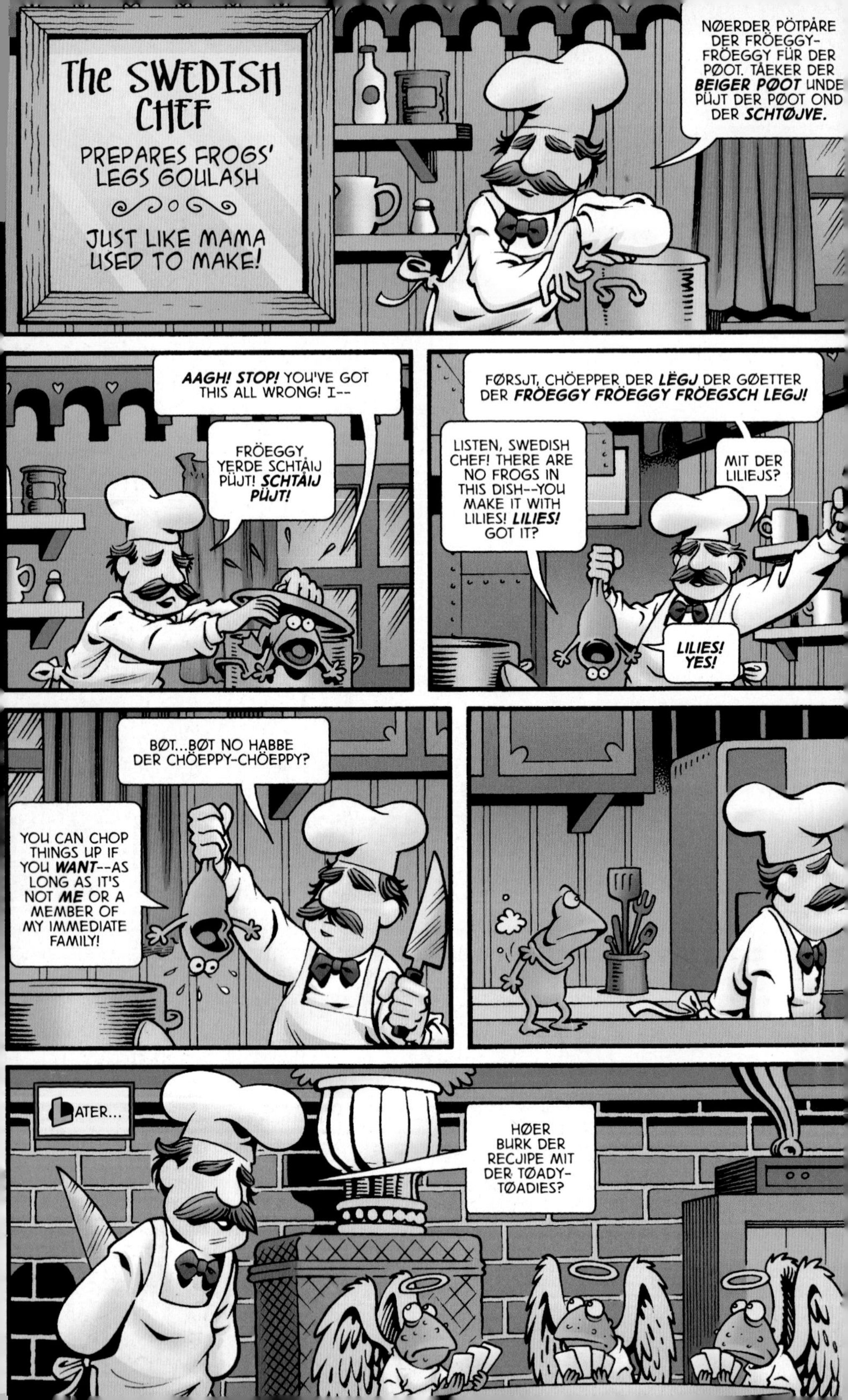
The SWEDISH CHEF
PREPARES FROGS' LEGS GOULASH
JUST LIKE MAMA USED TO MAKE!
NØERDER PÖTPÅRE DER FRÖEGGY-FRÖEGGY FÜR DER PØOT. TÅEKER DER BEIGER PØOT UNDE PÜJT DER PØOT OND DER SCHTØJVE.
AAGH! STOP! YOU'VE GOT THIS ALL WRONG! I--
FRÖEGGY YERDE SCHTÅIJ PÜJT! SCHTÅIJ PÜJT!
FØRSJT, CHÖEPPER DER LËGJ DER GØETTER DER FRÖEGGY FRÖEGGY FRÖEGSCH LEGJ!
LISTEN, SWEDISH CHEF! THERE ARE NO FROGS IN THIS DISH--YOU MAKE IT WITH LILIES! LILIES! GOT IT?
MIT DER LILIEJS?
LILIES! YES!
BØT...BØT NO HABBE DER CHÖEPPY-CHÖEPPY?
YOU CAN CHOP THINGS UP IF YOU WANT--AS LONG AS IT'S NOT ME OR A MEMBER OF MY IMMEDIATE FAMILY!
LATER...
HØER BURK DER RECJIPE MIT DER TØADY-TØADIES?

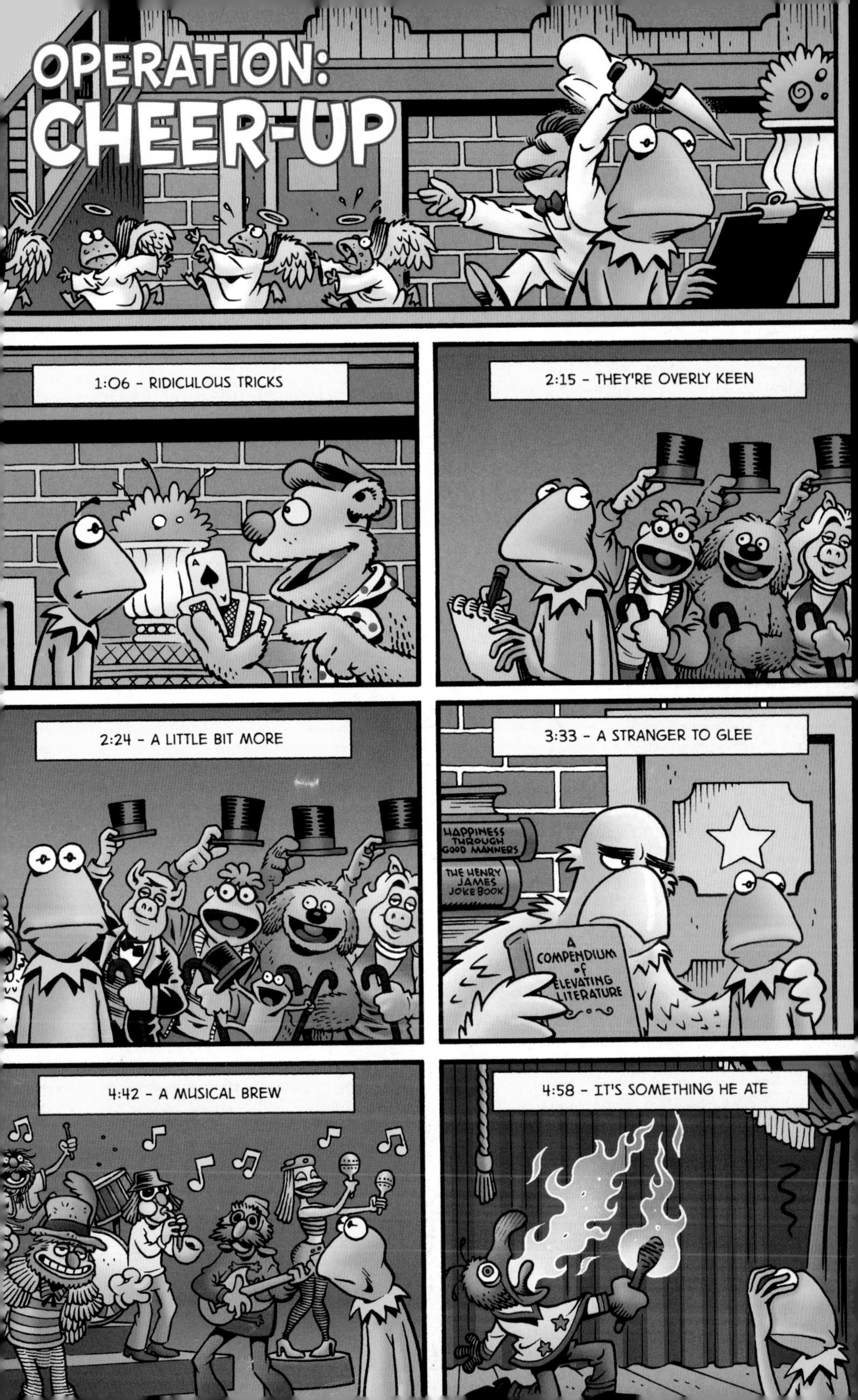
OPERATION: CHEER-UP
1:06 - RIDICULOUS TRICKS
2:15 - THEY'RE OVERLY KEEN
2:24 - A LITTLE BIT MORE
3:33 - A STRANGER TO GLEE
HAPPINESS THROUGH GOOD MANNERS
THE HENRY JAMES JOKE BOOK
A COMPENDIUM of ELEVATING LITERATURE
4:42 - A MUSICAL BREW
4:58 - IT'S SOMETHING HE ATE

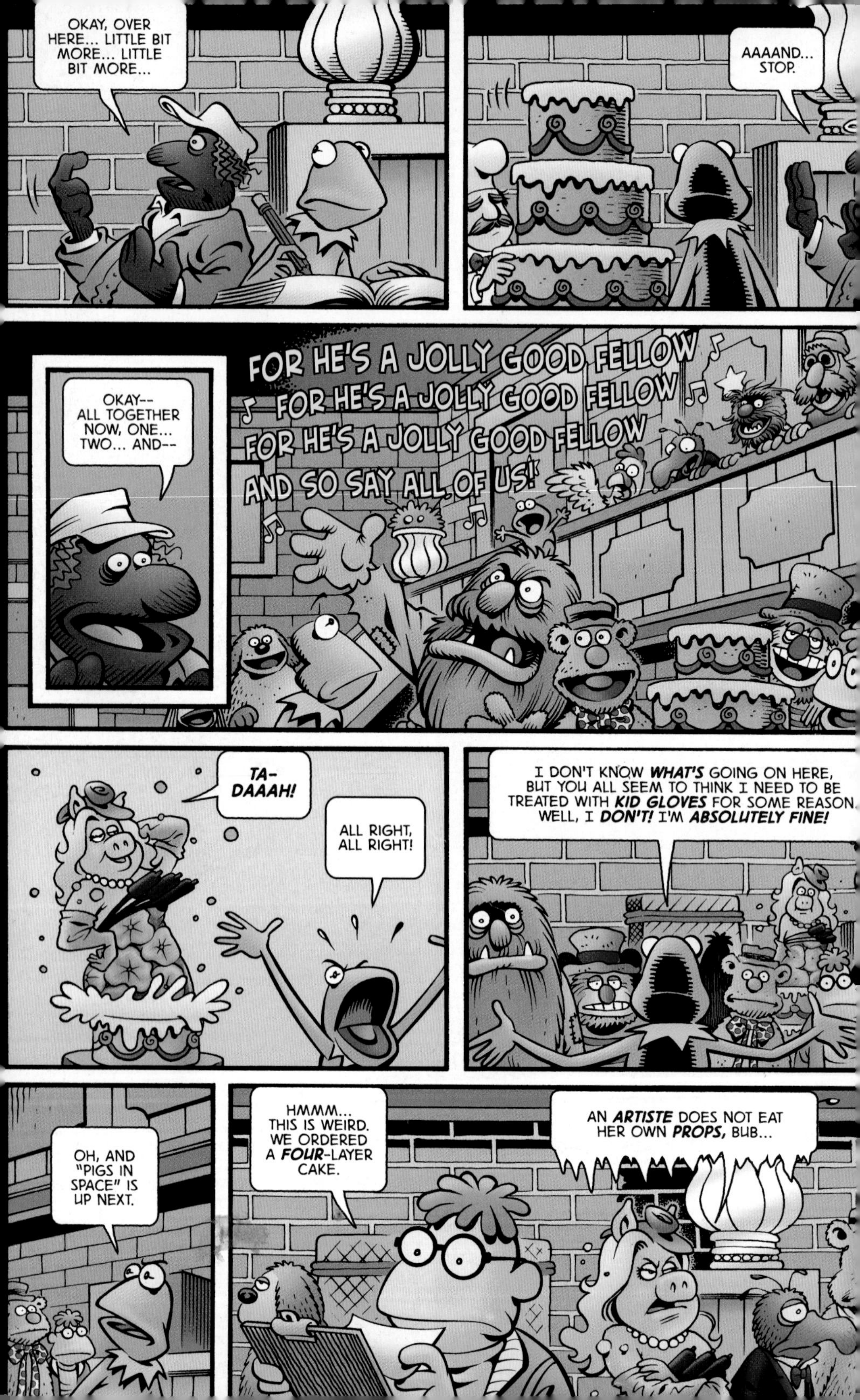

OKAY, OVER HERE... LITTLE BIT MORE... LITTLE BIT MORE...
AAAAND... STOP.
OKAY-- ALL TOGETHER NOW, ONE... TWO... AND--
FOR HE'S A JOLLY GOOD FELLOW
FOR HE'S A JOLLY GOOD FELLOW
FOR HE'S A JOLLY GOOD FELLOW
AND SO SAY ALL OF US!
TA-DAAAH!
ALL RIGHT, ALL RIGHT!
I DON'T KNOW WHAT'S GOING ON HERE, BUT YOU ALL SEEM TO THINK I NEED TO BE TREATED WITH KID GLOVES FOR SOME REASON. WELL, I DON'T! I'M ABSOLUTELY FINE!
OH, AND "PIGS IN SPACE" IS UP NEXT.
HMMM... THIS IS WEIRD. WE ORDERED A FOUR-LAYER CAKE.
AN ARTISTE DOES NOT EAT HER OWN PROPS, BUB...

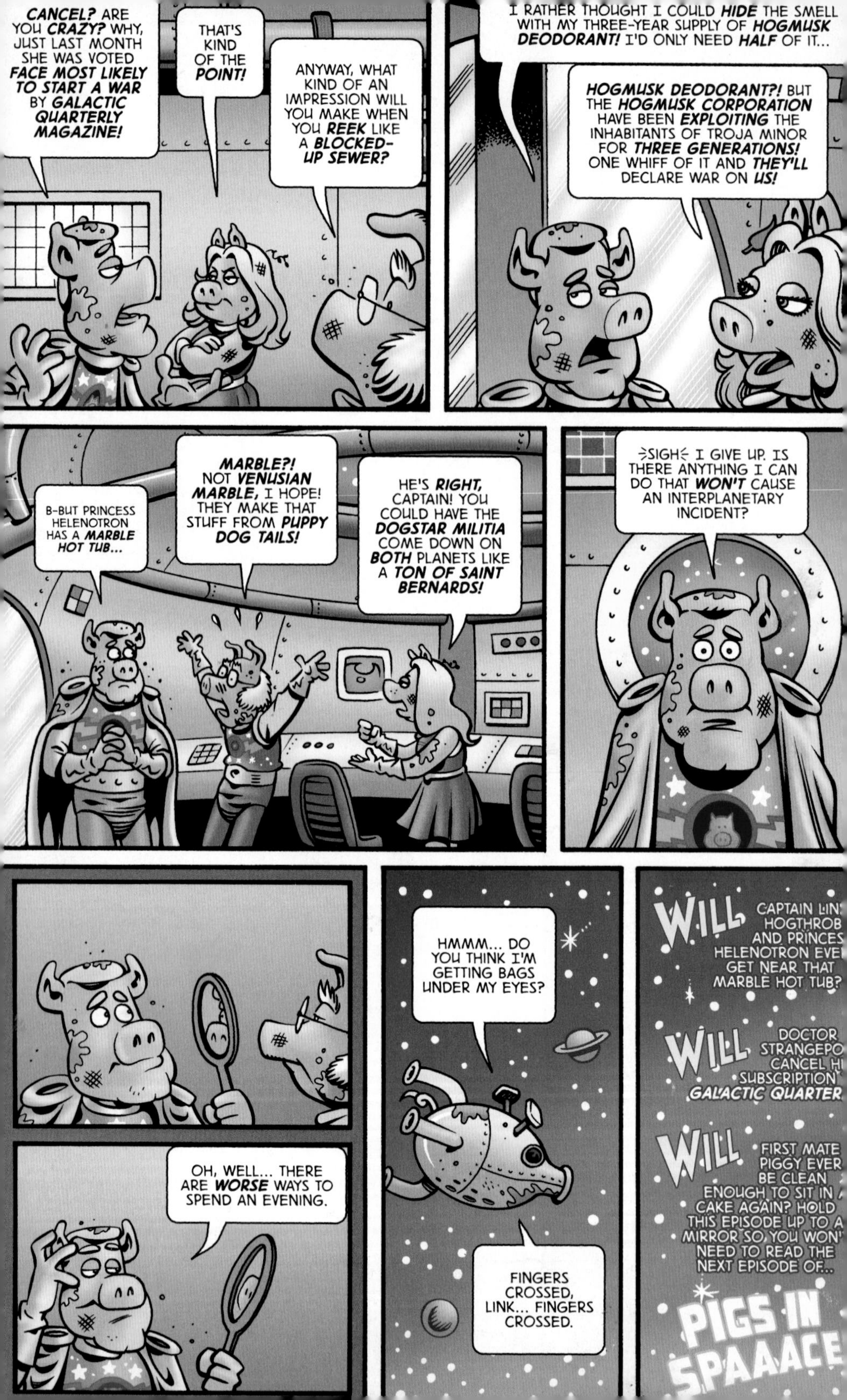
CANCEL? ARE YOU CRAZY? WHY, JUST LAST MONTH SHE WAS VOTED FACE MOST LIKELY TO START A WAR BY GALACTIC QUARTERLY MAGAZINE!
THAT'S KIND OF THE POINT!
ANYWAY, WHAT KIND OF AN IMPRESSION WILL YOU MAKE WHEN YOU REEK LIKE A BLOCKED-UP SEWER?
I RATHER THOUGHT I COULD HIDE THE SMELL WITH MY THREE-YEAR SUPPLY OF HOGMUSK DEODORANT! I'D ONLY NEED HALF OF IT...
HOGMUSK DEODORANT?! BUT THE HOGMUSK CORPORATION HAVE BEEN EXPLOITING THE INHABITANTS OF TROJA MINOR FOR THREE GENERATIONS! ONE WHIFF OF IT AND THEY'LL DECLARE WAR ON US!
B-BUT PRINCESS HELENOTRON HAS A MARBLE HOT TUB...
MARBLE?! NOT VENUSIAN MARBLE, I HOPE! THEY MAKE THAT STUFF FROM PUPPY DOG TAILS!
HE'S RIGHT, CAPTAIN! YOU COULD HAVE THE DOGSTAR MILITIA COME DOWN ON BOTH PLANETS LIKE A TON OF SAINT BERNARDS!
≯SIGH≮ I GIVE UP. IS THERE ANYTHING I CAN DO THAT WON'T CAUSE AN INTERPLANETARY INCIDENT?
OH, WELL... THERE ARE WORSE WAYS TO SPEND AN EVENING.
HMMM... DO YOU THINK I'M GETTING BAGS UNDER MY EYES?
FINGERS CROSSED, LINK... FINGERS CROSSED.
WILL CAPTAIN LIN HOGTHROB AND PRINCES HELENOTRON EVE GET NEAR THAT MARBLE HOT TUB?
WILL DOCTOR STRANGEPO CANCEL HI SUBSCRIPTION GALACTIC QUARTER
WILL FIRST MATE PIGGY EVER BE CLEAN ENOUGH TO SIT IN CAKE AGAIN? HOLD THIS EPISODE UP TO A MIRROR SO YOU WON NEED TO READ THE NEXT EPISODE OF...
PIGS IN SPAAACE

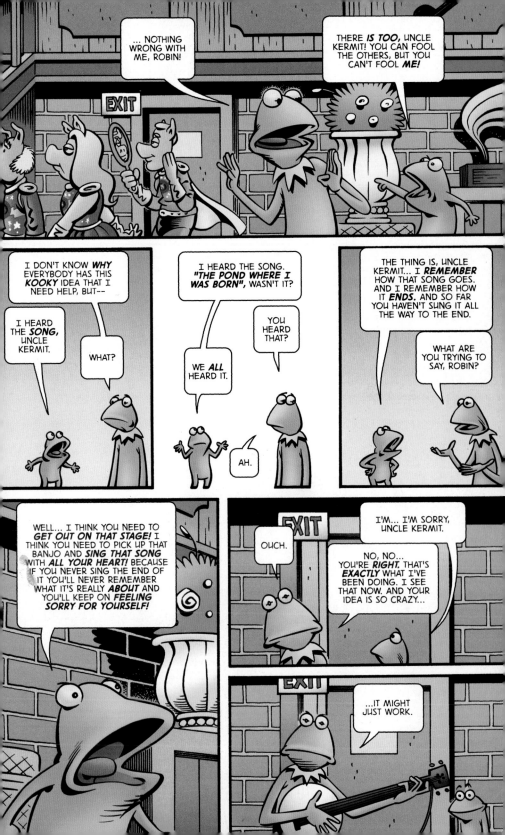

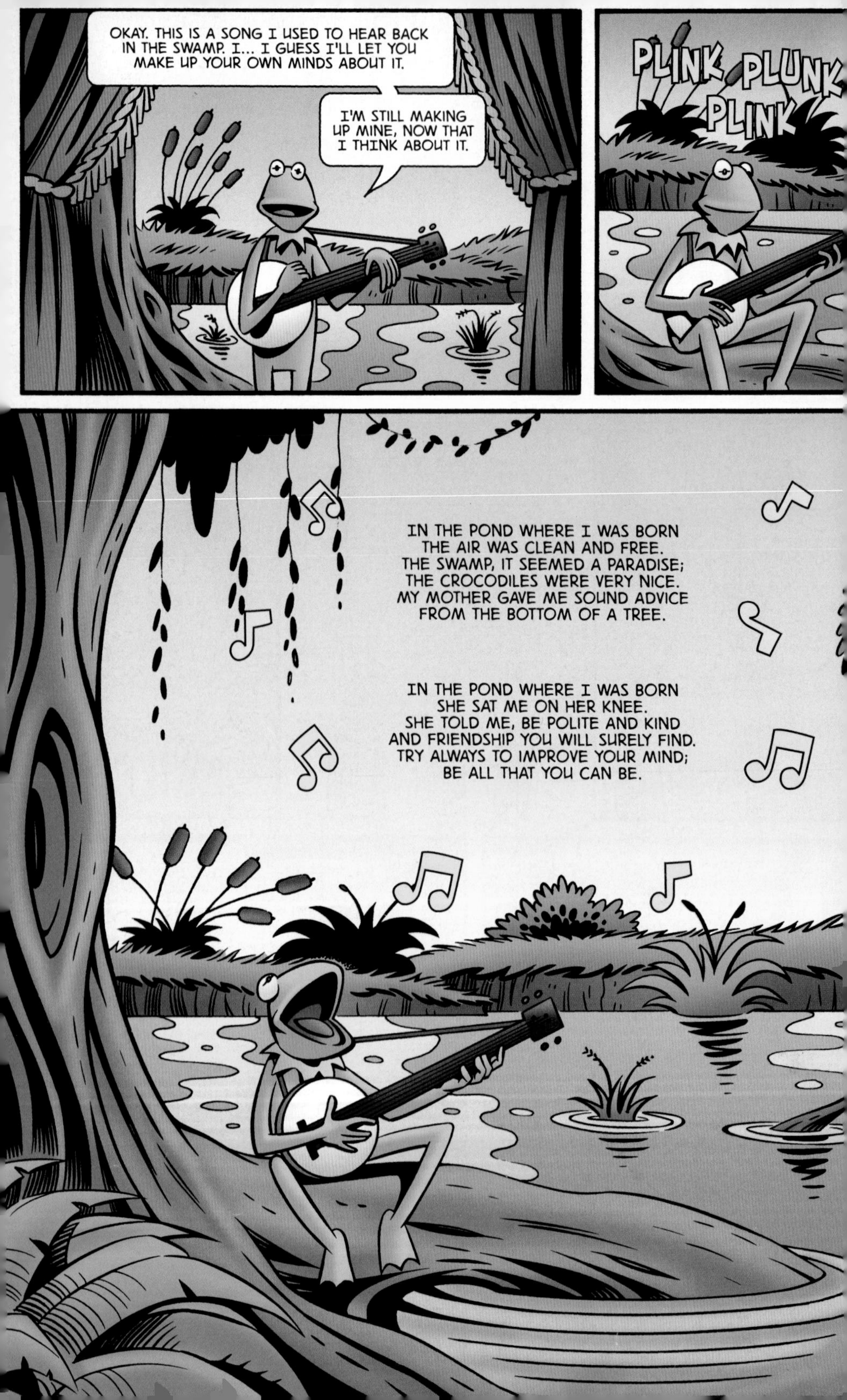
OKAY. THIS IS A SONG I USED TO HEAR BACK IN THE SWAMP. I... I GUESS I'LL LET YOU MAKE UP YOUR OWN MINDS ABOUT IT.
I'M STILL MAKING UP MINE, NOW THAT I THINK ABOUT IT.
PLINK PLUNK PLINK
IN THE POND WHERE I WAS BORN
THE AIR WAS CLEAN AND FREE.
THE SWAMP, IT SEEMED A PARADISE;
THE CROCODILES WERE VERY NICE.
MY MOTHER GAVE ME SOUND ADVICE
FROM THE BOTTOM OF A TREE.
IN THE POND WHERE I WAS BORN
SHE SAT ME ON HER KNEE.
SHE TOLD ME, BE POLITE AND KIND
AND FRIENDSHIP YOU WILL SURELY FIND.
TRY ALWAYS TO IMPROVE YOUR MIND;
BE ALL THAT YOU CAN BE.

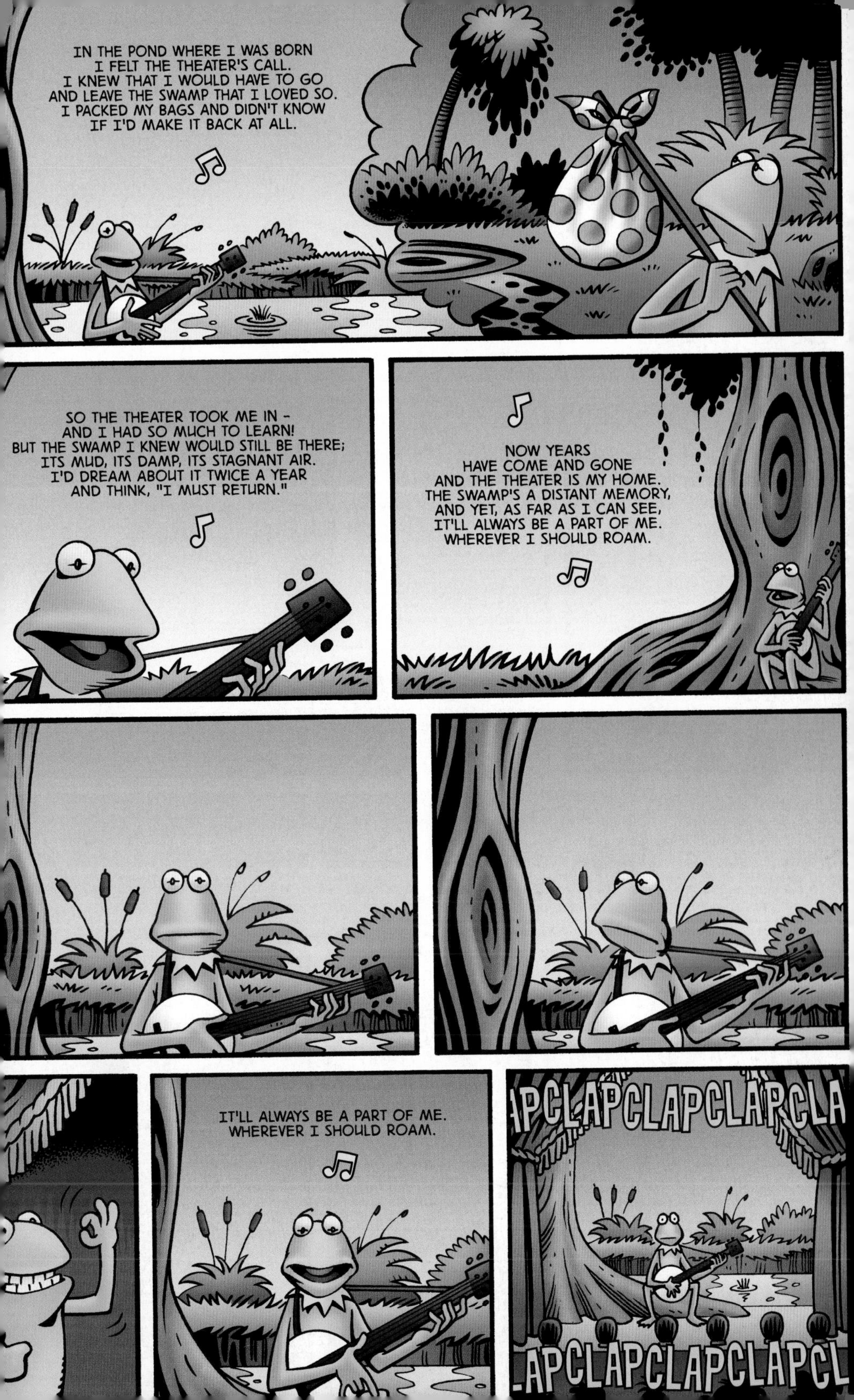
IN THE POND WHERE I WAS BORN
I FELT THE THEATER'S CALL.
I KNEW THAT I WOULD HAVE TO GO
AND LEAVE THE SWAMP THAT I LOVED SO.
I PACKED MY BAGS AND DIDN'T KNOW
IF I'D MAKE IT BACK AT ALL.
SO THE THEATER TOOK ME IN -
AND I HAD SO MUCH TO LEARN!
BUT THE SWAMP I KNEW WOULD STILL BE THERE;
ITS MUD, ITS DAMP, ITS STAGNANT AIR.
I'D DREAM ABOUT IT TWICE A YEAR
AND THINK, "I MUST RETURN."
NOW YEARS
HAVE COME AND GONE
AND THE THEATER IS MY HOME.
THE SWAMP'S A DISTANT MEMORY,
AND YET, AS FAR AS I CAN SEE,
IT'LL ALWAYS BE A PART OF ME.
WHEREVER I SHOULD ROAM.
IT'LL ALWAYS BE A PART OF ME.
WHEREVER I SHOULD ROAM.
APCLAPCLAPCLAPCLA
LAPCLAPCLAPCLAPCL

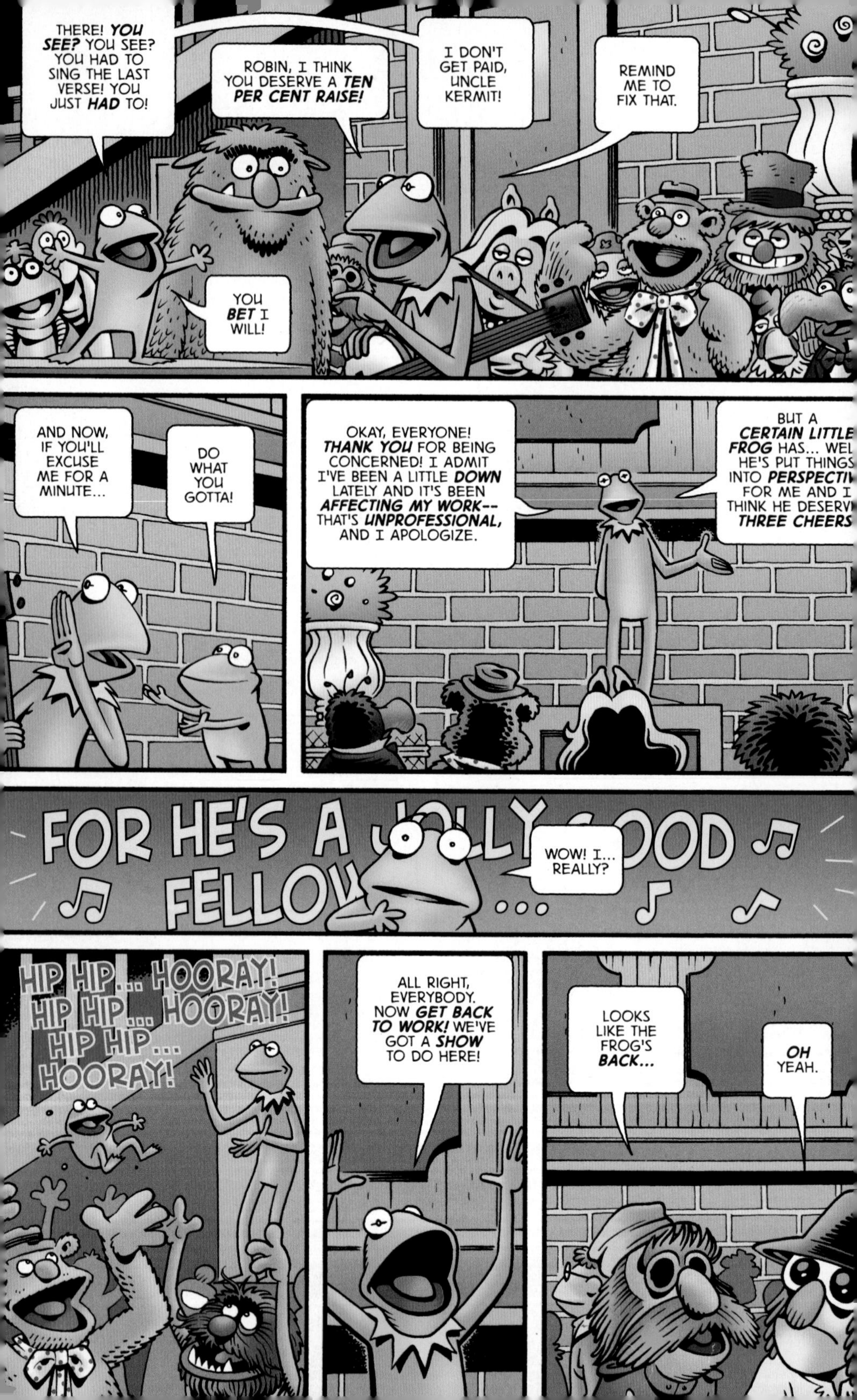
THERE! YOU SEE? YOU SEE? YOU HAD TO SING THE LAST VERSE! YOU JUST HAD TO!
ROBIN, I THINK YOU DESERVE A TEN PER CENT RAISE!
I DON'T GET PAID, UNCLE KERMIT!
REMIND ME TO FIX THAT.
YOU BET I WILL!
AND NOW, IF YOU'LL EXCUSE ME FOR A MINUTE...
DO WHAT YOU GOTTA!
OKAY, EVERYONE! THANK YOU FOR BEING CONCERNED! I ADMIT I'VE BEEN A LITTLE DOWN LATELY AND IT'S BEEN AFFECTING MY WORK-- THAT'S UNPROFESSIONAL, AND I APOLOGIZE.
BUT A CERTAIN LITTLE FROG HAS... WEL HE'S PUT THINGS INTO PERSPECTIV FOR ME AND I THINK HE DESERV THREE CHEERS
FOR HE'S A JOLLY GOOD FELLOW...
WOW! I... REALLY?
HIP HIP... HOORAY! HIP HIP... HOORAY! HIP HIP... HOORAY!
ALL RIGHT, EVERYBODY. NOW GET BACK TO WORK! WE'VE GOT A SHOW TO DO HERE!
LOOKS LIKE THE FROG'S BACK...
OH YEAH.

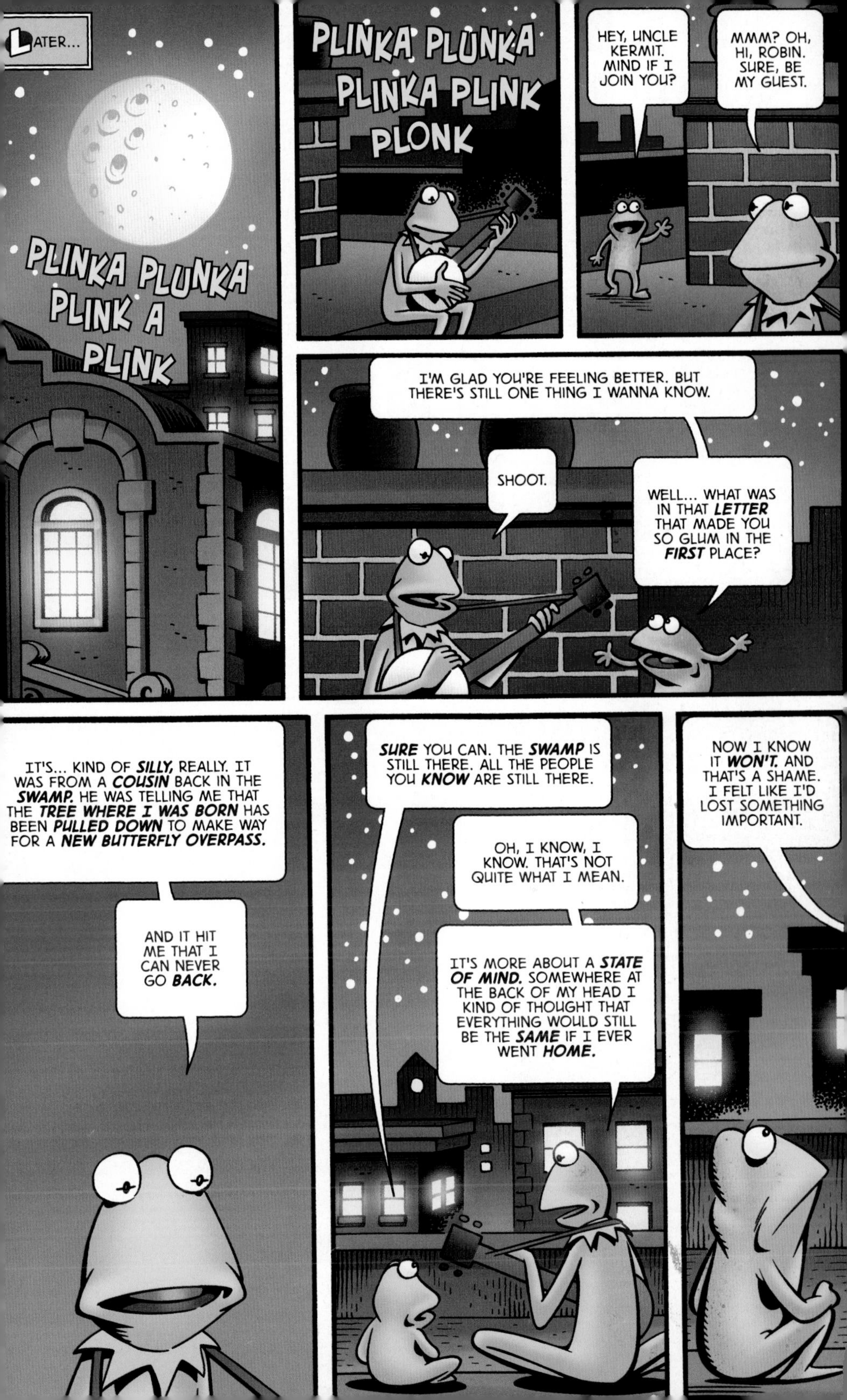
LATER...
PLINKA PLUNKA PLINK A PLINK
PLINKA PLUNKA PLINKA PLINK PLONK
HEY, UNCLE KERMIT. MIND IF I JOIN YOU?
MMM? OH, HI, ROBIN. SURE, BE MY GUEST.
I'M GLAD YOU'RE FEELING BETTER. BUT THERE'S STILL ONE THING I WANNA KNOW.
SHOOT.
WELL... WHAT WAS IN THAT LETTER THAT MADE YOU SO GLUM IN THE FIRST PLACE?
IT'S... KIND OF SILLY, REALLY. IT WAS FROM A COUSIN BACK IN THE SWAMP. HE WAS TELLING ME THAT THE TREE WHERE I WAS BORN HAS BEEN PULLED DOWN TO MAKE WAY FOR A NEW BUTTERFLY OVERPASS.
AND IT HIT ME THAT I CAN NEVER GO BACK.
SURE YOU CAN. THE SWAMP IS STILL THERE. ALL THE PEOPLE YOU KNOW ARE STILL THERE.
OH, I KNOW, I KNOW. THAT'S NOT QUITE WHAT I MEAN.
IT'S MORE ABOUT A STATE OF MIND. SOMEWHERE AT THE BACK OF MY HEAD I KIND OF THOUGHT THAT EVERYTHING WOULD STILL BE THE SAME IF I EVER WENT HOME.
NOW I KNOW IT WON'T. AND THAT'S A SHAME. I FELT LIKE I'D LOST SOMETHING IMPORTANT.

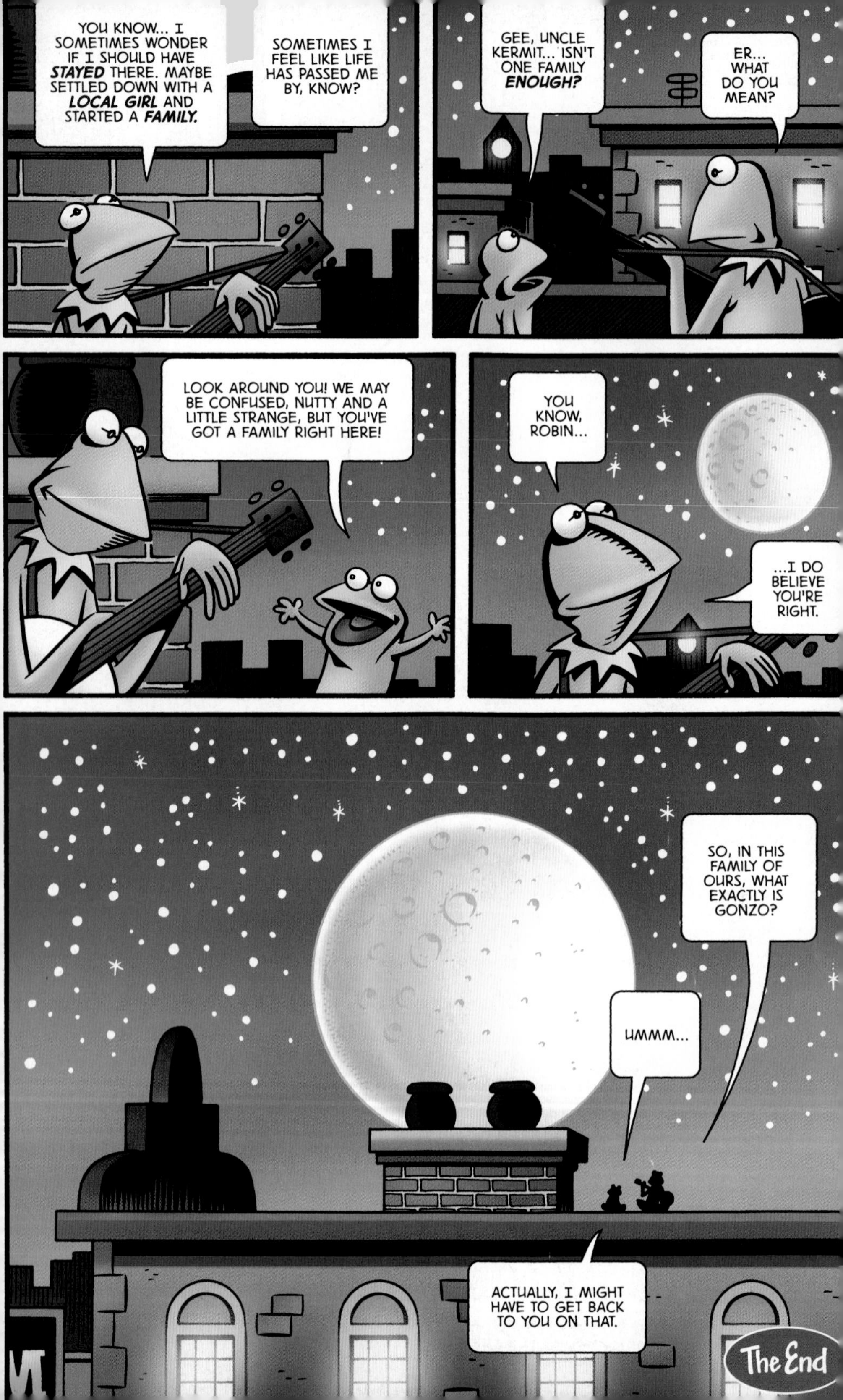
YOU KNOW... I SOMETIMES WONDER IF I SHOULD HAVE STAYED THERE. MAYBE SETTLED DOWN WITH A LOCAL GIRL AND STARTED A FAMILY.
SOMETIMES I FEEL LIKE LIFE HAS PASSED ME BY, KNOW?
GEE, UNCLE KERMIT... ISN'T ONE FAMILY ENOUGH?
ER... WHAT DO YOU MEAN?
LOOK AROUND YOU! WE MAY BE CONFUSED, NUTTY AND A LITTLE STRANGE, BUT YOU'VE GOT A FAMILY RIGHT HERE!
YOU KNOW, ROBIN...
...I DO BELIEVE YOU'RE RIGHT.
SO, IN THIS FAMILY OF OURS, WHAT EXACTLY IS GONZO?
UMMM...
ACTUALLY, I MIGHT HAVE TO GET BACK TO YOU ON THAT.
The End

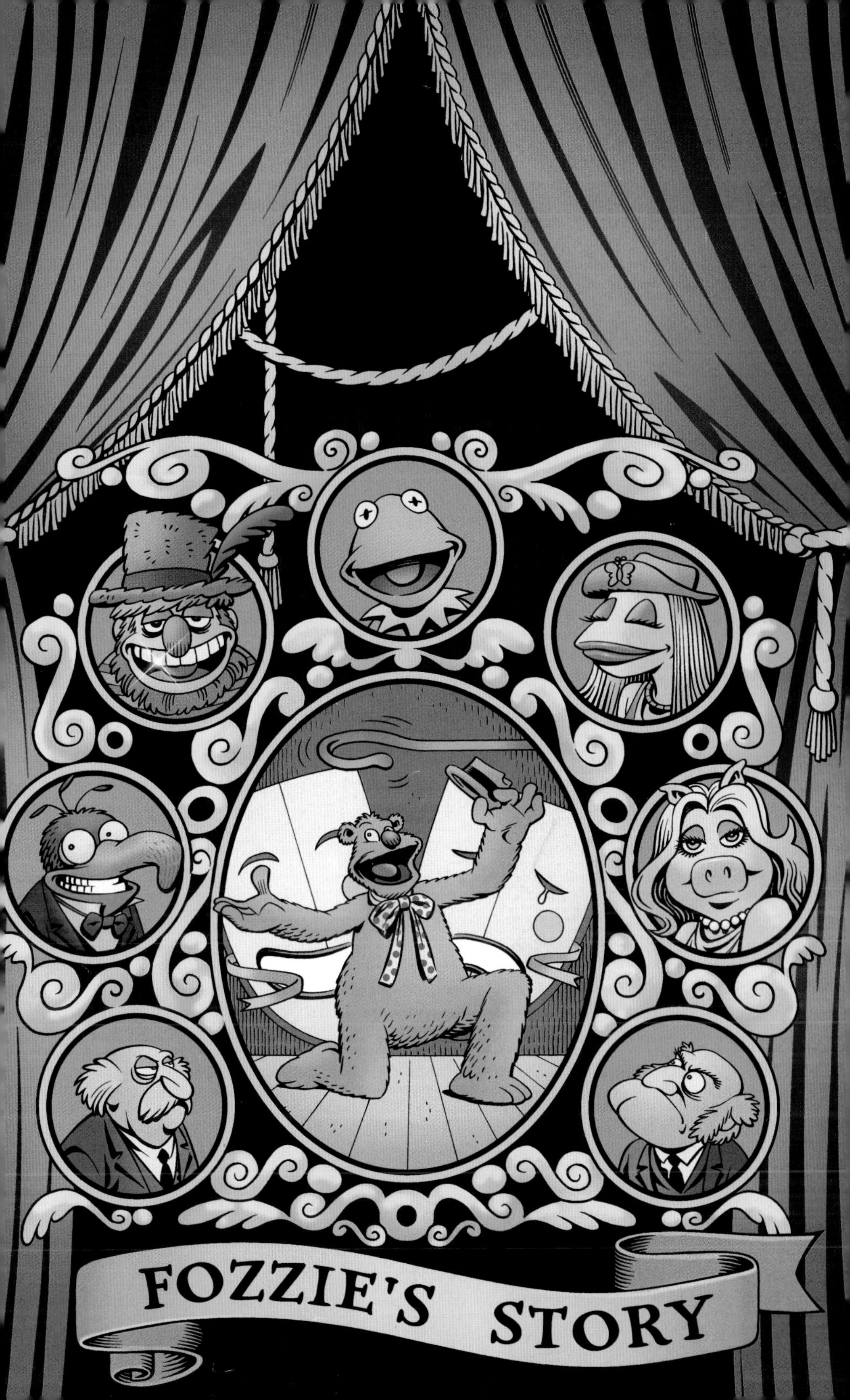
FOZZIE'S STORY

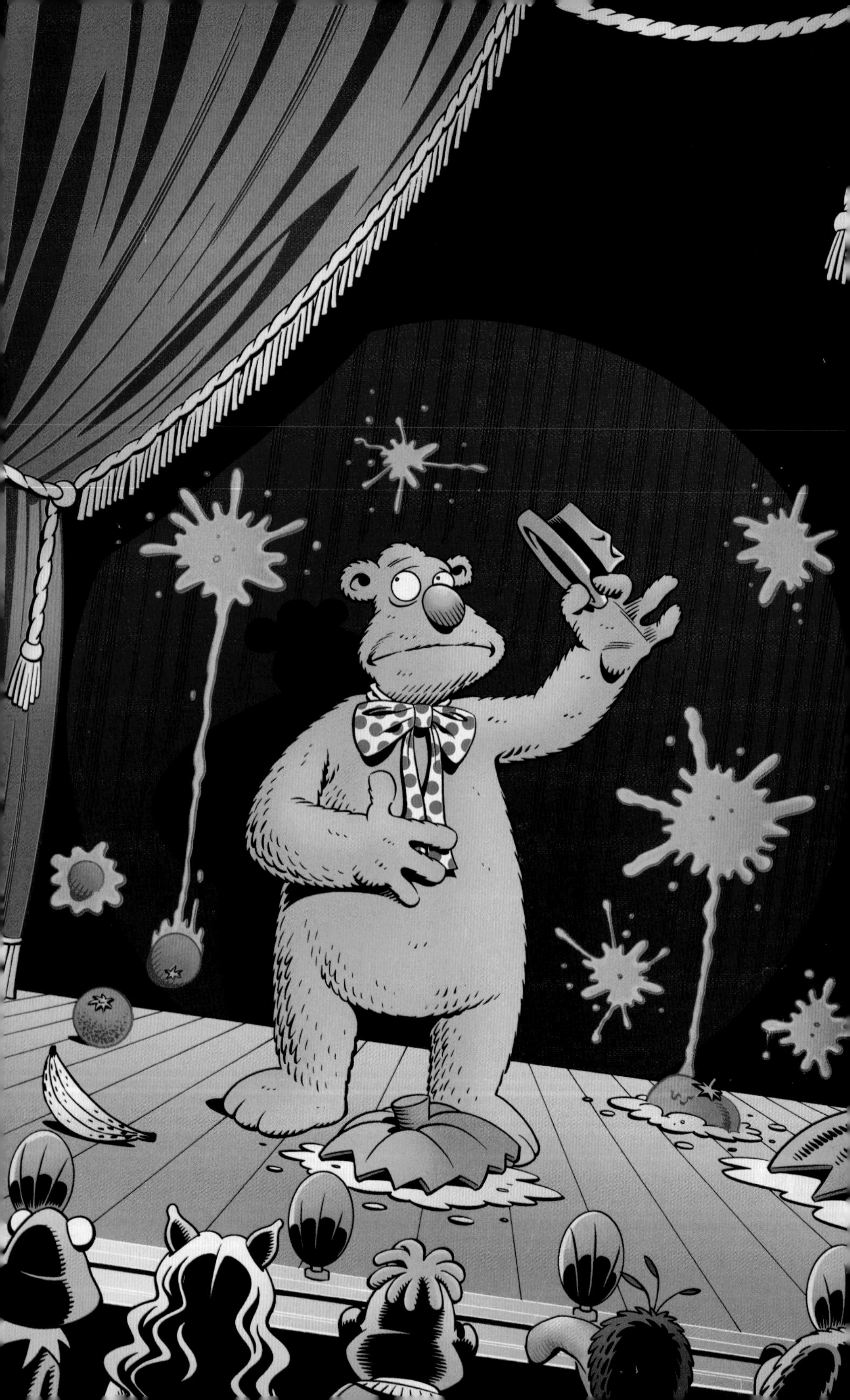

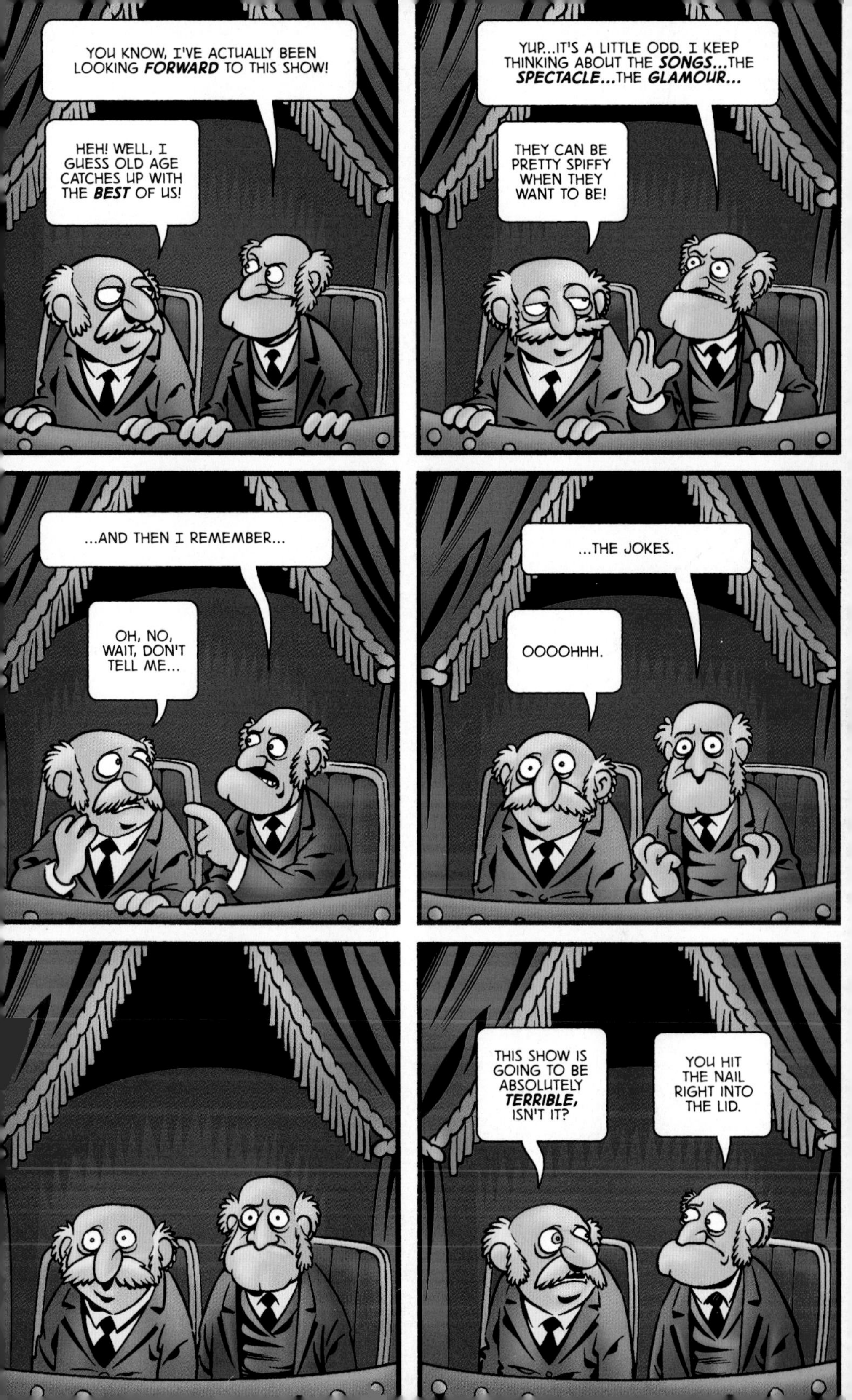
YOU KNOW, I'VE ACTUALLY BEEN LOOKING **FORWARD** TO THIS SHOW!
HEH! WELL, I GUESS OLD AGE CATCHES UP WITH THE **BEST** OF US!
YUP...IT'S A LITTLE ODD. I KEEP THINKING ABOUT THE **SONGS...**THE **SPECTACLE...**THE **GLAMOUR...**
THEY CAN BE PRETTY SPIFFY WHEN THEY WANT TO BE!
...AND THEN I REMEMBER...
OH, NO, WAIT, DON'T TELL ME...
...THE JOKES.
OOOOHHH.
THIS SHOW IS GOING TO BE ABSOLUTELY **TERRIBLE,** ISN'T IT?
YOU HIT THE NAIL RIGHT INTO THE LID.

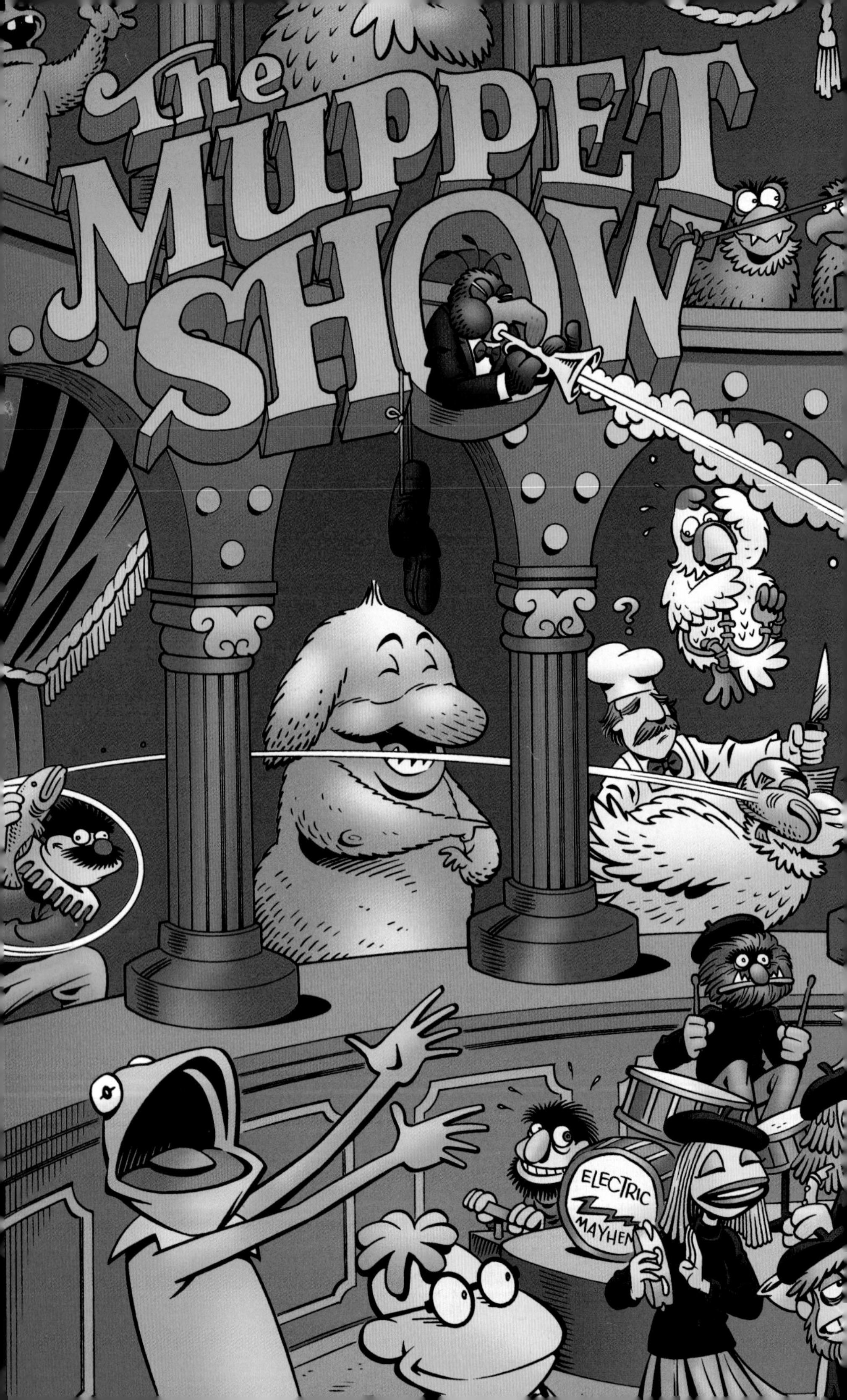
The MUPPET SHOW
?
ELECTRIC MAYHEM

AHAAA! *YES!* SO THIS *GORILLA* WALKS THROUGH THE DOOR, AND HE GOES UP TO THE COUNTER AND SHOUTS, *"THREE POUNDS OF LIMBURGER CHEESE, PLEASE!"* AND THE LADY BEHIND THE COUNTER GOES, "SIR, I'M AFRAID THIS IS A LIBRARY."

SO THE GORILLA LOOKS EMBARRASSED AND WHISPERS:

"I'M SORRY. THREE POUNDS OF LIMBURGER CHEESE, PLEASE."

NICE WORK, GUYS! ALMOST PROFESSIONAL STANDARD THIS TIME! LOSE THE CASUAL VIOLENCE AND WE MIGHT YET **MAKE** IT.

OH, KERMIT. OH MY OH MY OH MY.

THEY **HATED** ME. **HATED ME!** TELL ME, KERMIT-- AS A FRIEND--DO YOU THINK I'VE LOST MY **TOUCH?**

HONESTLY?

I WOULDN'T **WORRY** IF I WERE YOU. I JUST THINK YOU WERE PUSHING IT WITH THE **CHEESE GAGS.** WE'VE GOT A CROWD FROM THE **CHEESE MANUFACTURERS' CONVENTION** OUT THERE-- THEY'RE A **SENSITIVE BUNCH.**

OH, KERMIT! I WISH IT WERE THAT **SIMPLE!**

NO... I'M CONVINCED THAT MY ACT NEEDS TO BE **REINVENTED** FROM **FIRST PRINCIPLES!** IF MY OLD SET ISN'T **GOOD** ENOUGH FOR THEM, I'LL JUST HAVE TO FIND **ANOTHER** ONE!

WELL, I'LL LEAVE IT TO YOU, FOZZIE. I'M SURE YOU KNOW WHAT YOU'RE DOING.

LATER...

AAGHH! I WISH I KNEW WHAT I WAS **DOING!**

FOZZIE BEAR

÷SIGH÷ MAYBE THE OL' **LIBRARY** HAS A CLUE OR TWO. I NEED **INSPIRATION!**

OHO! **AHA!** YES! **YES!** MAYBE I DON'T KNOW WHAT I'M DOING--BUT NOBODY COULD EVER SAY THAT **WILLIAM SHAKESPEARE** WASN'T FUNNY!

WHERE'S MY NOTEBOOK? I'VE GOT A **SET** TO WRITE!

NEXT:

IN MY MERRY

OLDSMOBIL

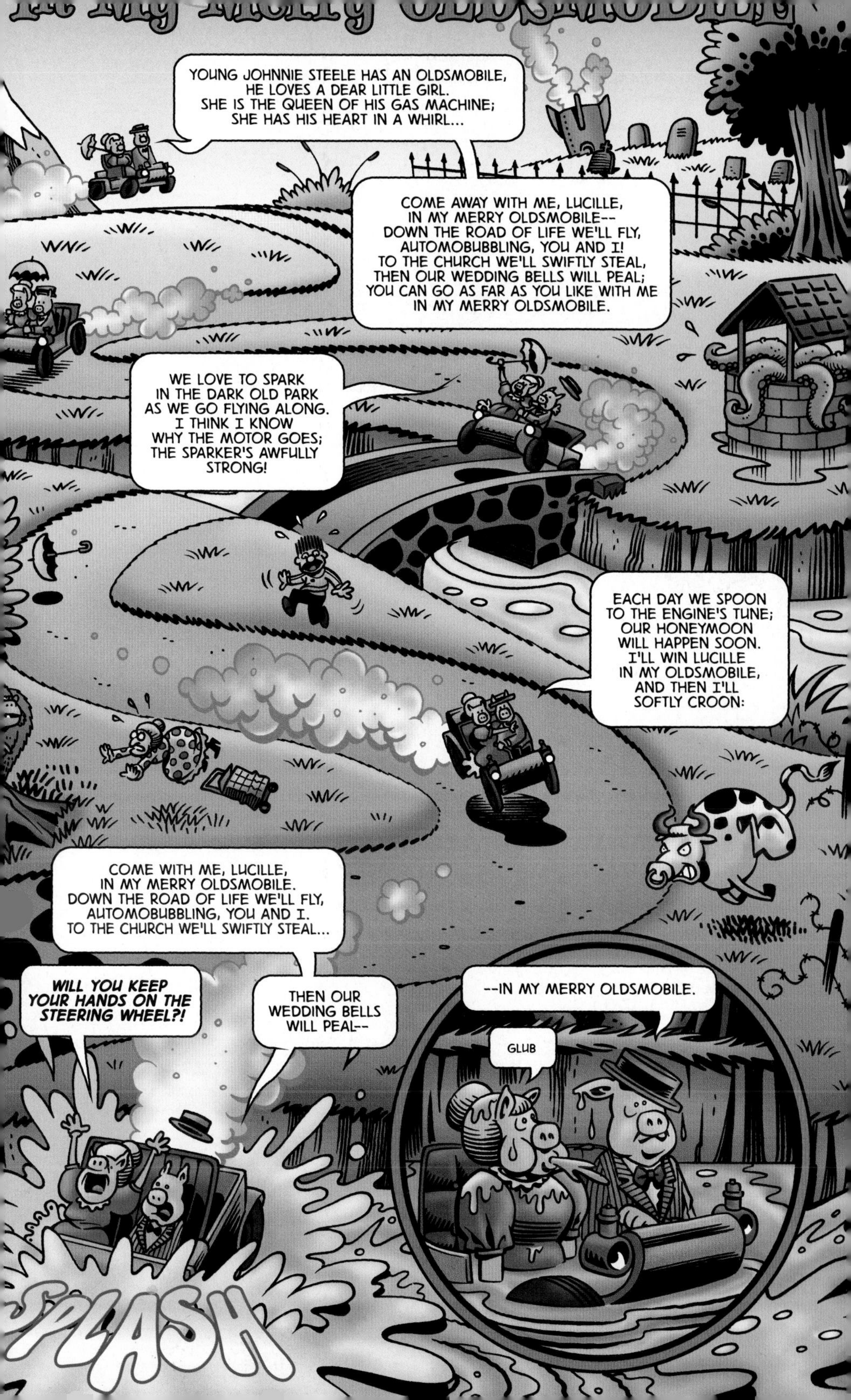
YOUNG JOHNNIE STEELE HAS AN OLDSMOBILE, HE LOVES A DEAR LITTLE GIRL. SHE IS THE QUEEN OF HIS GAS MACHINE; SHE HAS HIS HEART IN A WHIRL...
COME AWAY WITH ME, LUCILLE, IN MY MERRY OLDSMOBILE-- DOWN THE ROAD OF LIFE WE'LL FLY, AUTOMOBUBBLING, YOU AND I! TO THE CHURCH WE'LL SWIFTLY STEAL, THEN OUR WEDDING BELLS WILL PEAL; YOU CAN GO AS FAR AS YOU LIKE WITH ME IN MY MERRY OLDSMOBILE.
WE LOVE TO SPARK IN THE DARK OLD PARK AS WE GO FLYING ALONG. I THINK I KNOW WHY THE MOTOR GOES; THE SPARKER'S AWFULLY STRONG!
EACH DAY WE SPOON TO THE ENGINE'S TUNE; OUR HONEYMOON WILL HAPPEN SOON. I'LL WIN LUCILLE IN MY OLDSMOBILE, AND THEN I'LL SOFTLY CROON:
COME WITH ME, LUCILLE, IN MY MERRY OLDSMOBILE. DOWN THE ROAD OF LIFE WE'LL FLY, AUTOMOBUBBLING, YOU AND I. TO THE CHURCH WE'LL SWIFTLY STEAL...
WILL YOU KEEP YOUR HANDS ON THE STEERING WHEEL?!
THEN OUR WEDDING BELLS WILL PEAL--
--IN MY MERRY OLDSMOBILE.
GLUB
SPLASH

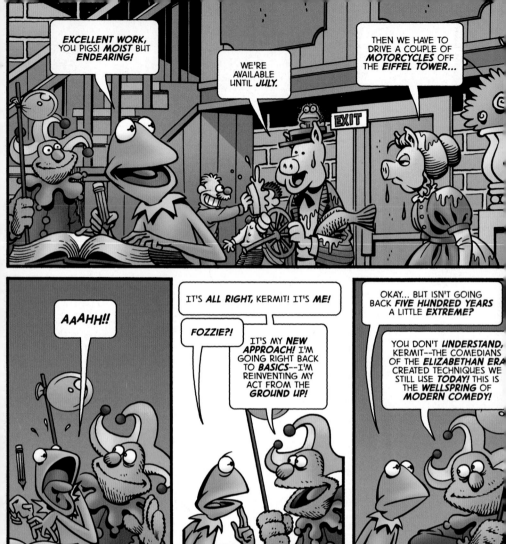

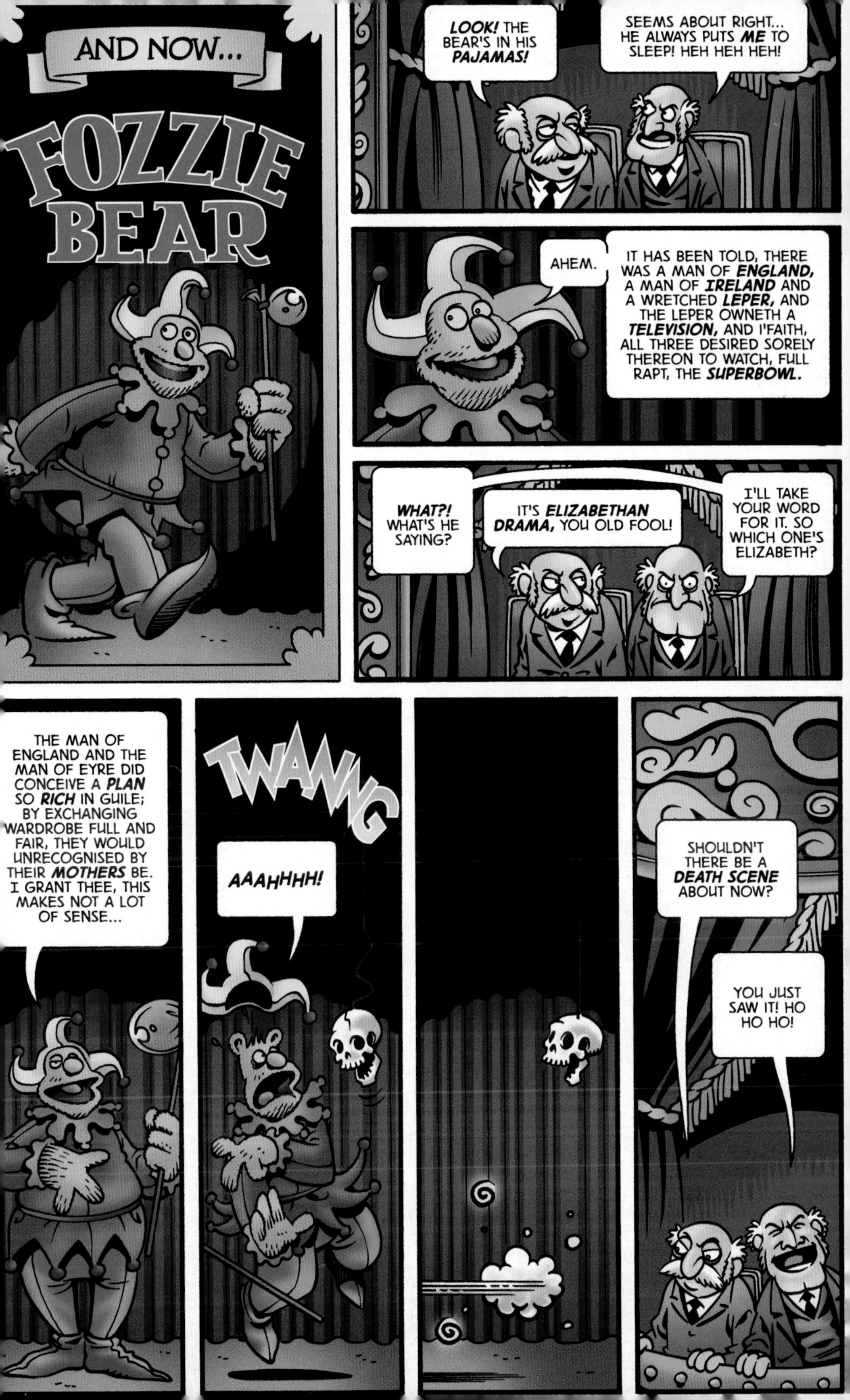
AND NOW...
FOZZIE BEAR
LOOK! THE BEAR'S IN HIS PAJAMAS!
SEEMS ABOUT RIGHT... HE ALWAYS PUTS ME TO SLEEP! HEH HEH HEH!
AHEM.
IT HAS BEEN TOLD, THERE WAS A MAN OF ENGLAND, A MAN OF IRELAND AND A WRETCHED LEPER, AND THE LEPER OWNETH A TELEVISION, AND I'FAITH, ALL THREE DESIRED SORELY THEREON TO WATCH, FULL RAPT, THE SUPERBOWL.
WHAT?! WHAT'S HE SAYING?
IT'S ELIZABETHAN DRAMA, YOU OLD FOOL!
I'LL TAKE YOUR WORD FOR IT. SO WHICH ONE'S ELIZABETH?
THE MAN OF ENGLAND AND THE MAN OF EYRE DID CONCEIVE A PLAN SO RICH IN GUILE; BY EXCHANGING WARDROBE FULL AND FAIR, THEY WOULD UNRECOGNISED BY THEIR MOTHERS BE. I GRANT THEE, THIS MAKES NOT A LOT OF SENSE...
TWANNG
AAAHHHH!
SHOULDN'T THERE BE A DEATH SCENE ABOUT NOW?
YOU JUST SAW IT! HO HO HO!

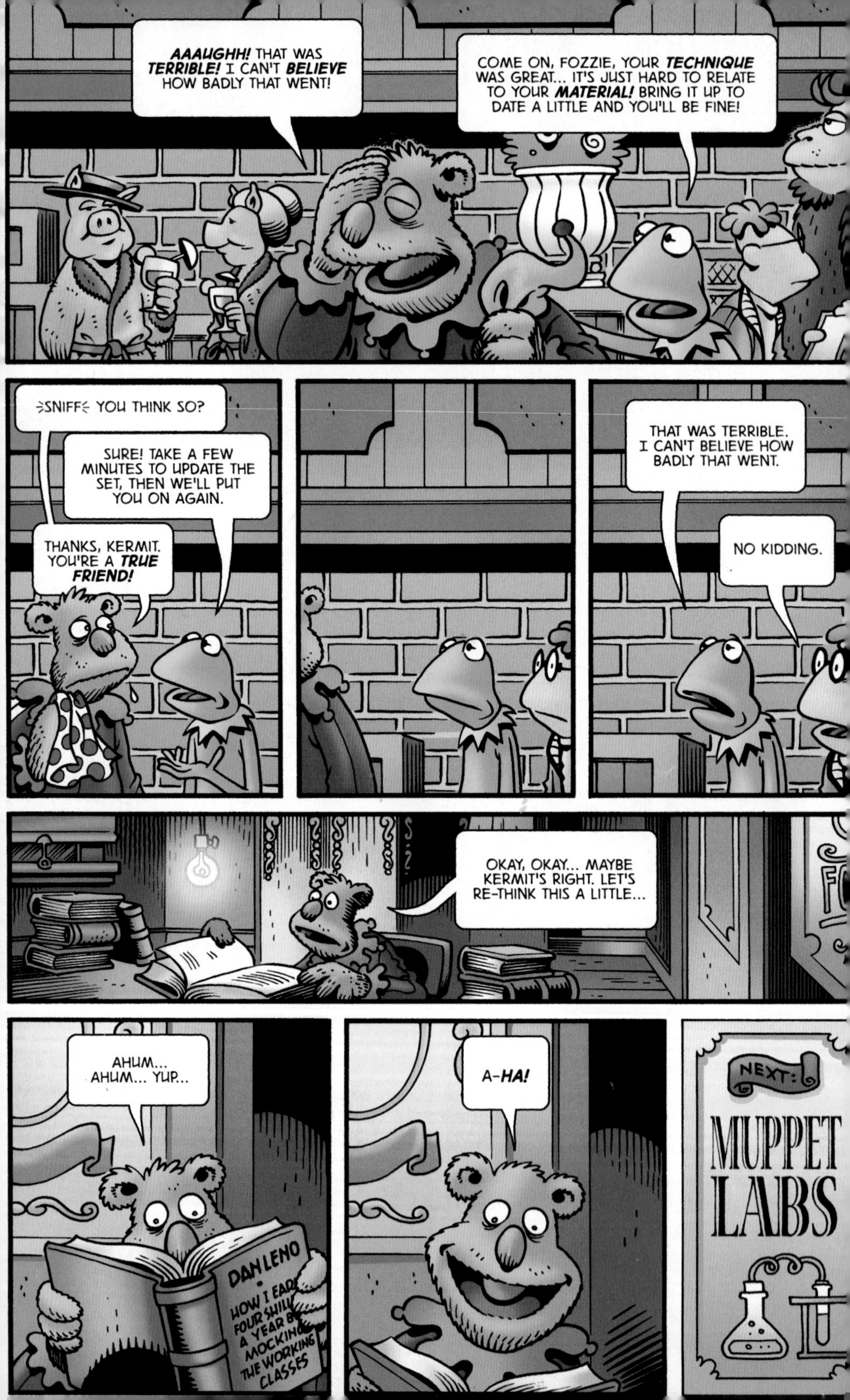
AAAUGHH! THAT WAS TERRIBLE! I CAN'T BELIEVE HOW BADLY THAT WENT!
COME ON, FOZZIE, YOUR TECHNIQUE WAS GREAT... IT'S JUST HARD TO RELATE TO YOUR MATERIAL! BRING IT UP TO DATE A LITTLE AND YOU'LL BE FINE!
≥SNIFF≤ YOU THINK SO?
SURE! TAKE A FEW MINUTES TO UPDATE THE SET, THEN WE'LL PUT YOU ON AGAIN.
THANKS, KERMIT. YOU'RE A TRUE FRIEND!
THAT WAS TERRIBLE. I CAN'T BELIEVE HOW BADLY THAT WENT.
NO KIDDING.
OKAY, OKAY... MAYBE KERMIT'S RIGHT. LET'S RE-THINK THIS A LITTLE...
AHUM... AHUM... YUP...
DAN LENO
A-HA!
NEXT:
MUPPET LABS

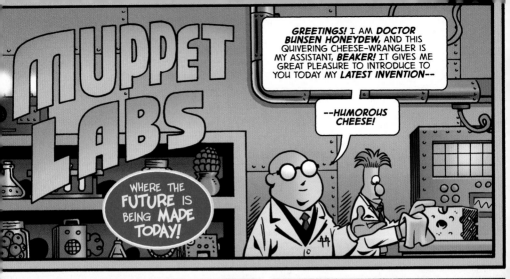

MUPPET LABS

WHERE THE FUTURE IS BEING MADE TODAY!

GREETINGS! I AM DOCTOR BUNSEN HONEYDEW, AND THIS QUIVERING CHEESE-WRANGLER IS MY ASSISTANT, BEAKER! IT GIVES ME GREAT PLEASURE TO INTRODUCE TO YOU TODAY MY LATEST INVENTION--

--HUMOROUS CHEESE!

THE PRINCIPLE IS SIMPLE! THIS CHEESE CAME FROM COWS WITH A GREATER THAN AVERAGE SENSE OF HUMOR!

THE CHEESE HAS THEN BEEN AGED TO GET IT TO A POINT WHERE IT'S READY TO WALK OUT THE DOOR BY ITSELF...

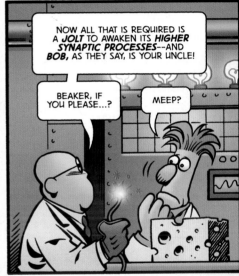

NOW ALL THAT IS REQUIRED IS A JOLT TO AWAKEN ITS HIGHER SYNAPTIC PROCESSES--AND BOB, AS THEY SAY, IS YOUR UNCLE!

BEAKER, IF YOU PLEASE...?

MEEP?

IF MY THEORY IS ACCURATE, THIS CHEESE WILL EMERGE FROM OUR PROCEDURE WITH SPEECH, HIGHER BRAIN FUNCTIONS AND EXCELLENT CAREER PROSPECTS!

M-MEEP! MEEP! MEEEEPPP!!

ZZZAAPPP!

HEY THERE! HEY THERE! WHAT HAS EIGHT WHEELS AND FLIES? TWO PICKUP TRUCKS FULL OF LIMBURGER! HAH! I GOT A MILLION OF 'EM!

MEEP MEEP MEEP MEEP MEEP

SUCCESS!!

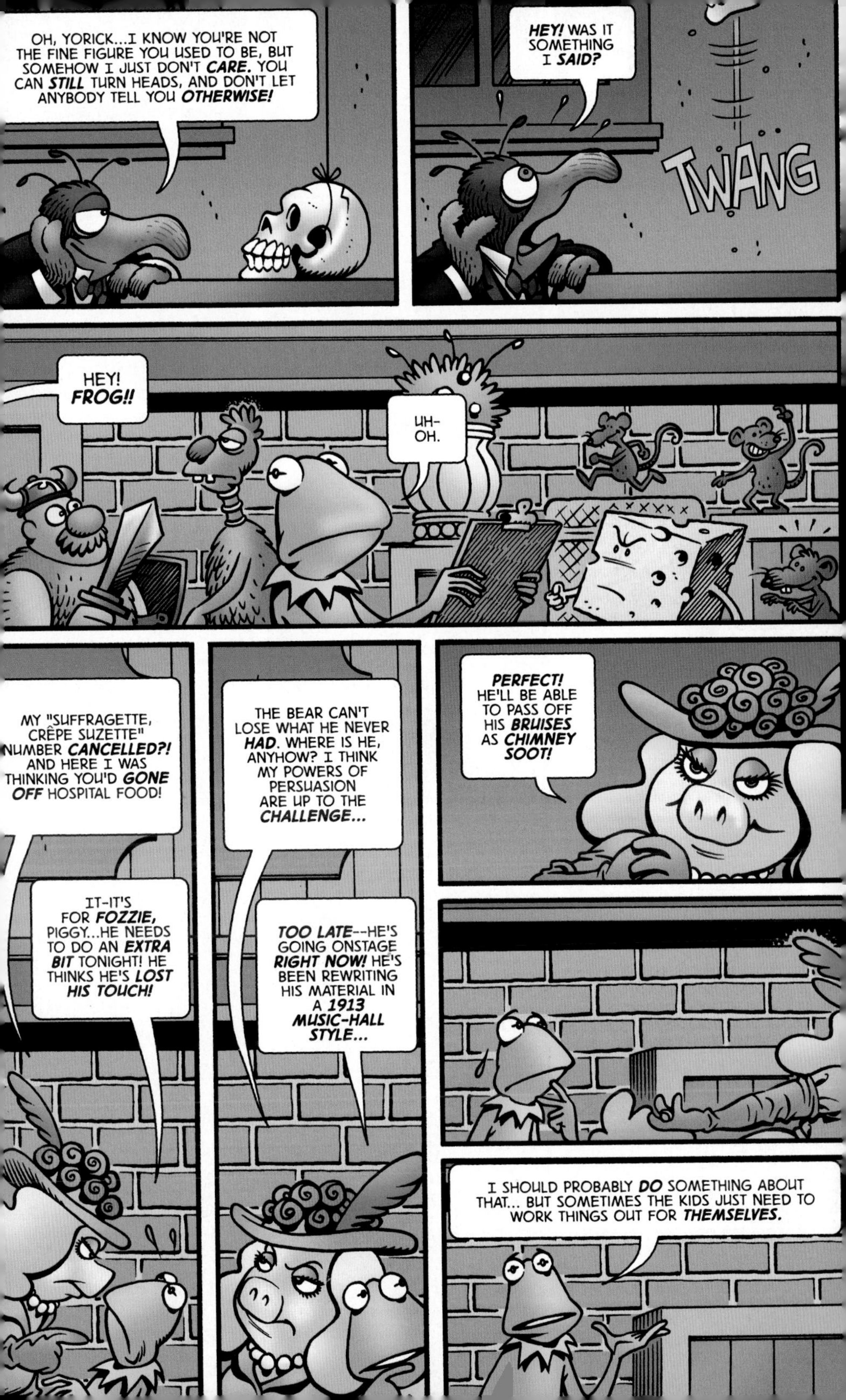
OH, YORICK...I KNOW YOU'RE NOT THE FINE FIGURE YOU USED TO BE, BUT SOMEHOW I JUST DON'T CARE. YOU CAN STILL TURN HEADS, AND DON'T LET ANYBODY TELL YOU OTHERWISE!
HEY! WAS IT SOMETHING I SAID?
TWANG
HEY! FROG!!
UH-OH.
MY "SUFFRAGETTE, CRÊPE SUZETTE" NUMBER CANCELLED?! AND HERE I WAS THINKING YOU'D GONE OFF HOSPITAL FOOD!
IT-IT'S FOR FOZZIE, PIGGY...HE NEEDS TO DO AN EXTRA BIT TONIGHT! HE THINKS HE'S LOST HIS TOUCH!
THE BEAR CAN'T LOSE WHAT HE NEVER HAD. WHERE IS HE, ANYHOW? I THINK MY POWERS OF PERSUASION ARE UP TO THE CHALLENGE...
TOO LATE--HE'S GOING ONSTAGE RIGHT NOW! HE'S BEEN REWRITING HIS MATERIAL IN A 1913 MUSIC-HALL STYLE...
PERFECT! HE'LL BE ABLE TO PASS OFF HIS BRUISES AS CHIMNEY SOOT!
I SHOULD PROBABLY DO SOMETHING ABOUT THAT... BUT SOMETIMES THE KIDS JUST NEED TO WORK THINGS OUT FOR THEMSELVES.

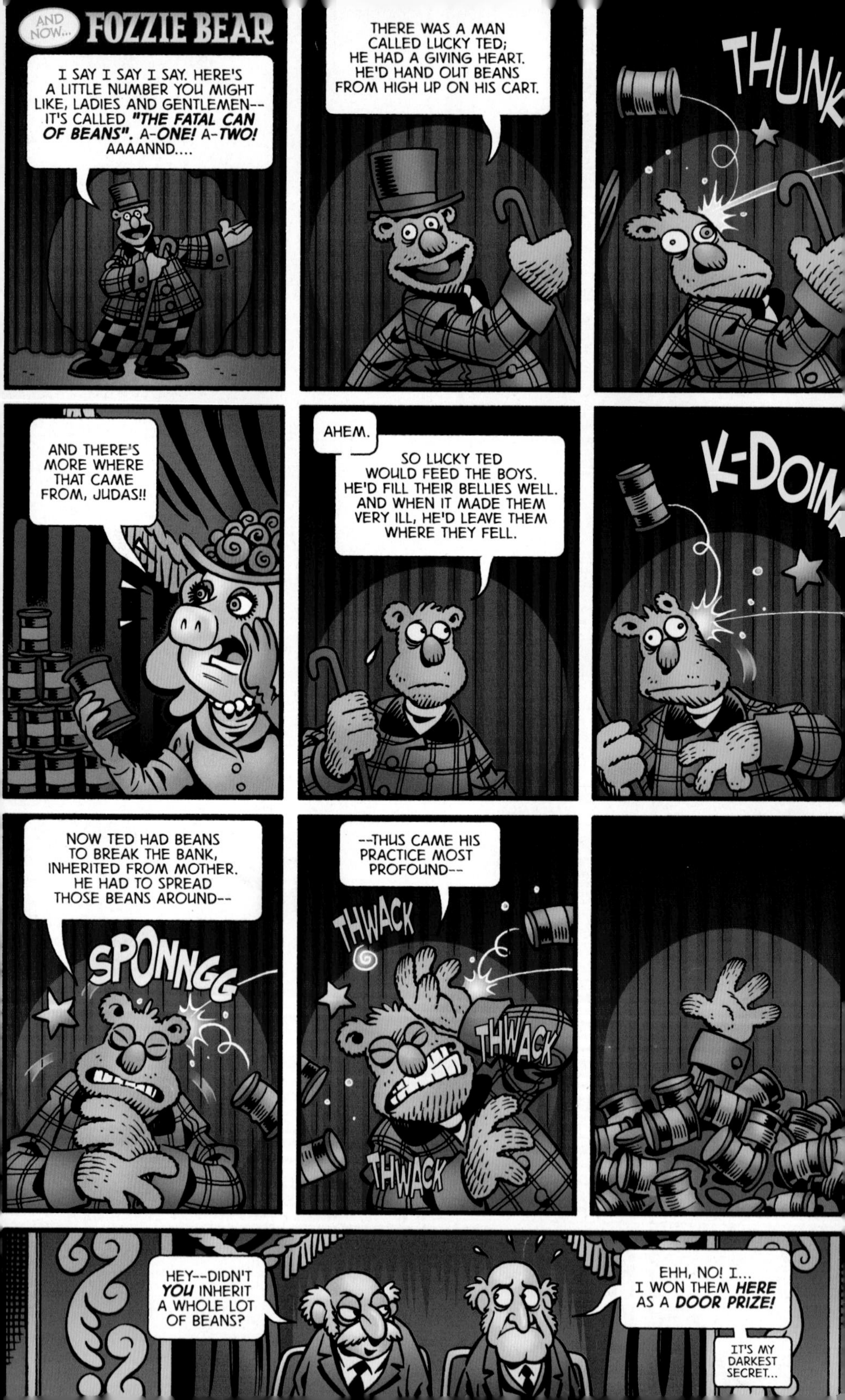
AND NOW... FOZZIE BEAR
I SAY I SAY I SAY. HERE'S A LITTLE NUMBER YOU MIGHT LIKE, LADIES AND GENTLEMEN-- IT'S CALLED "THE FATAL CAN OF BEANS". A-ONE! A-TWO! AAAANND....
THERE WAS A MAN CALLED LUCKY TED; HE HAD A GIVING HEART. HE'D HAND OUT BEANS FROM HIGH UP ON HIS CART.
THUNK
AND THERE'S MORE WHERE THAT CAME FROM, JUDAS!!
AHEM.
SO LUCKY TED WOULD FEED THE BOYS. HE'D FILL THEIR BELLIES WELL. AND WHEN IT MADE THEM VERY ILL, HE'D LEAVE THEM WHERE THEY FELL.
K-DOIN
NOW TED HAD BEANS TO BREAK THE BANK, INHERITED FROM MOTHER. HE HAD TO SPREAD THOSE BEANS AROUND--
SPONNGG
--THUS CAME HIS PRACTICE MOST PROFOUND--
THWACK
THWACK
THWACK
HEY--DIDN'T YOU INHERIT A WHOLE LOT OF BEANS?
EHH, NO! I... I WON THEM HERE AS A DOOR PRIZE!
IT'S MY DARKEST SECRET...

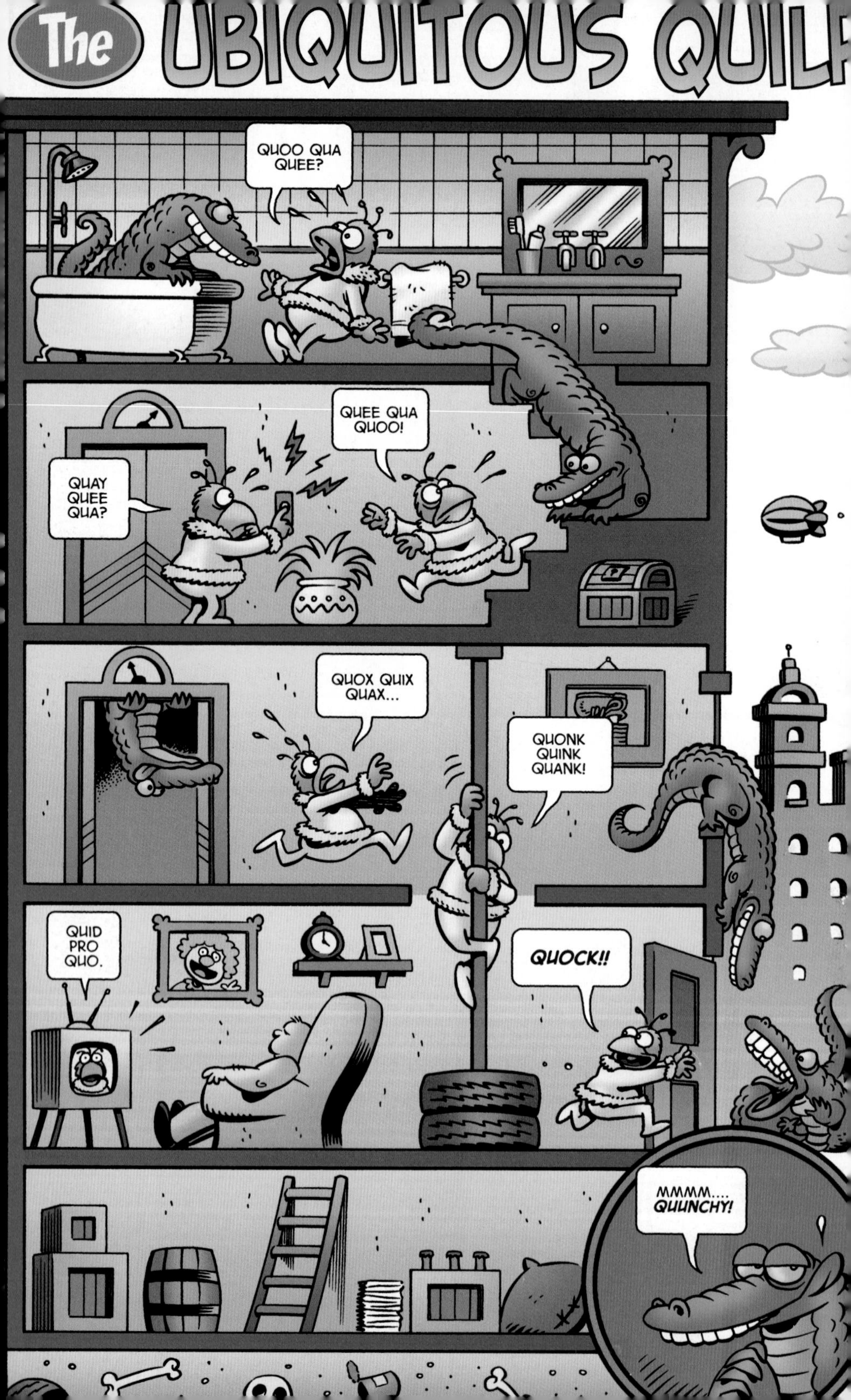
The UBIQUITOUS QUIL
QUOO QUA QUEE?
QUAY QUEE QUA?
QUEE QUA QUOO!
QUOX QUIX QUAX...
QUONK QUINK QUANK!
QUID PRO QUO.
QUOCK!!
MMMM.... QUUNCHY!

ALL RIGHT, NURSE JANICE...WHAT'S THE DIAGNOSIS?

IT'S, LIKE, THAT *THING* YOU DO WHEN YOU TRY TO WORK OUT WHAT'S WRONG WITH THE *PATIENT?*

BOY, ARE *YOU* IN THE WRONG PROFESSION!

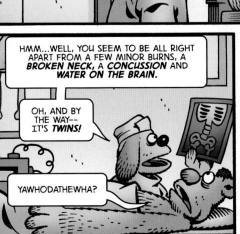

HMM...WELL, YOU SEEM TO BE ALL RIGHT APART FROM A FEW MINOR BURNS, A *BROKEN NECK*, A *CONCUSSION* AND *WATER ON THE BRAIN.*

OH, AND BY THE WAY-- IT'S *TWINS!*

YAWHODATHEWHA?

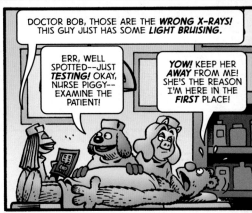

DOCTOR BOB, THOSE ARE THE *WRONG X-RAYS!* THIS GUY JUST HAS SOME *LIGHT BRUISING.*

ERR, WELL SPOTTED--JUST *TESTING!* OKAY, NURSE PIGGY-- EXAMINE THE PATIENT!

YOW! KEEP HER *AWAY* FROM ME! SHE'S THE REASON I'M HERE IN THE *FIRST* PLACE!

NURSE PIGGY! IS THIS TRUE?

MY HANDS SLIPPED.

THIRTY-SEVEN TIMES?!

I'M *VERY* CLUMSY.

BUT...BUT I DON'T *PLAY* THE VIOLIN.

OH. IN THAT CASE, YOU'VE ONLY GOT *THREE DAYS TO LIVE!*

HA HA HA HA HA HA

I'M JUST KIDDING! I GIVE YOU AT *LEAST* A MONTH!

GREAT! WELL, NO EVIDENCE OF MALPRACTICE HERE! WE'LL HAVE YOU BACK PLAYING THAT VIOLIN IN *NO TIME!*

WILL DOCTOR BOB REVIVE HIS FAILING BEDSIDE MANNER? WILL NURSE PIGGY GET TO SEE ONE OF THOSE NICE PSYCHOLOGISTS EVERYONE'S TALKING ABOUT? WILL FOZZIE LEARN THE VIOLIN, JUST FOR KICKS? TUNE IN NEXT TIME, WHEN YOU CAN HEAR FOZZIE SAY...

SO TELL ME STRAIGHT, DOC... WILL I BE *OKAY?*

YOU'LL BE FINE...BUT THOSE *TWINS* ARE GOING TO KEEP YOU UP *ALL NIGHT!*

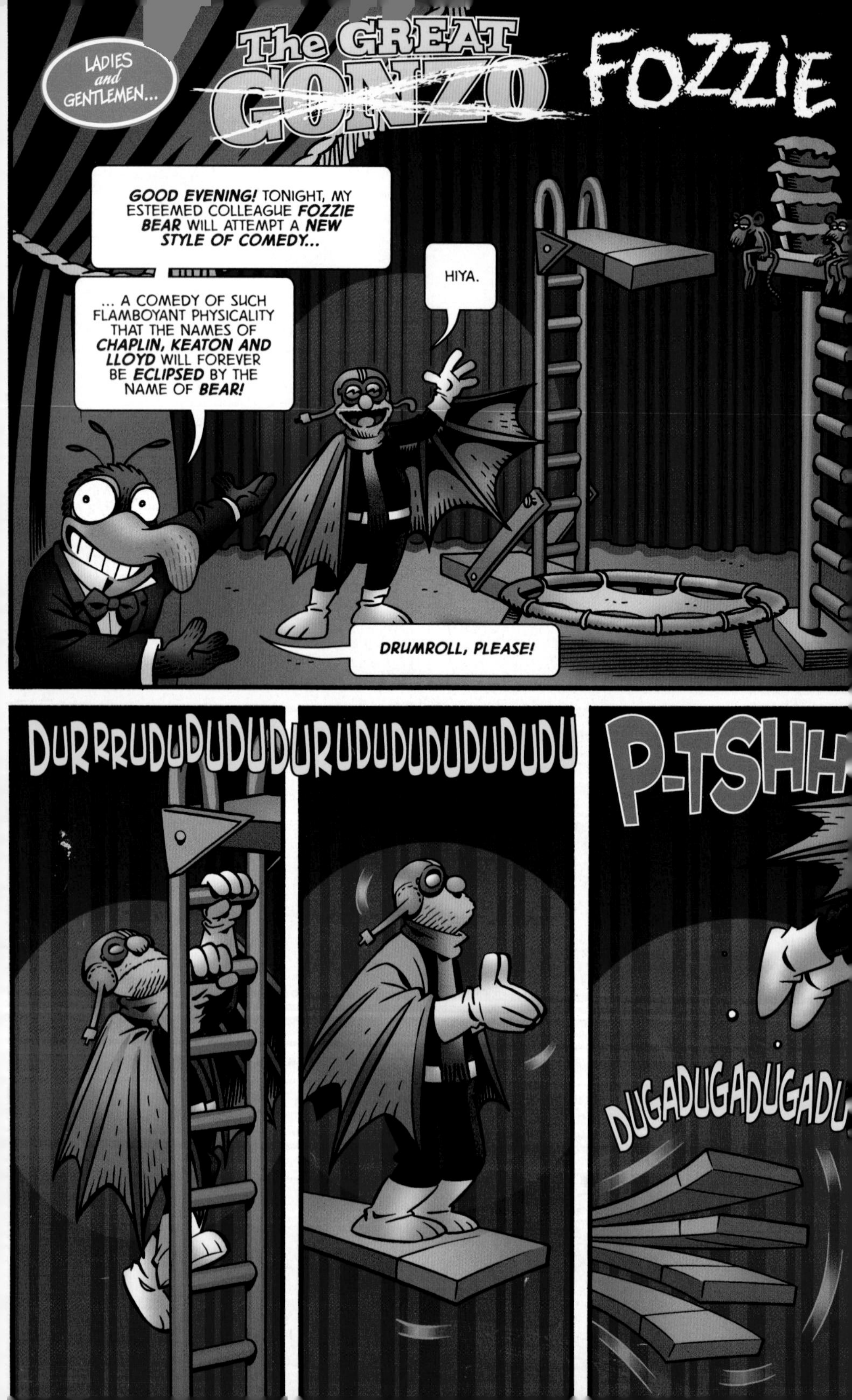
LADIES and GENTLEMEN...
The GREAT GONZO
FOZZIE
GOOD EVENING! TONIGHT, MY ESTEEMED COLLEAGUE FOZZIE BEAR WILL ATTEMPT A NEW STYLE OF COMEDY...
... A COMEDY OF SUCH FLAMBOYANT PHYSICALITY THAT THE NAMES OF CHAPLIN, KEATON AND LLOYD WILL FOREVER BE ECLIPSED BY THE NAME OF BEAR!
HIYA.
DRUMROLL, PLEASE!
DURRRUDUDUDUDURUDUDUDUDUDUDU
P-TSHH
DUGADUGADUGADU

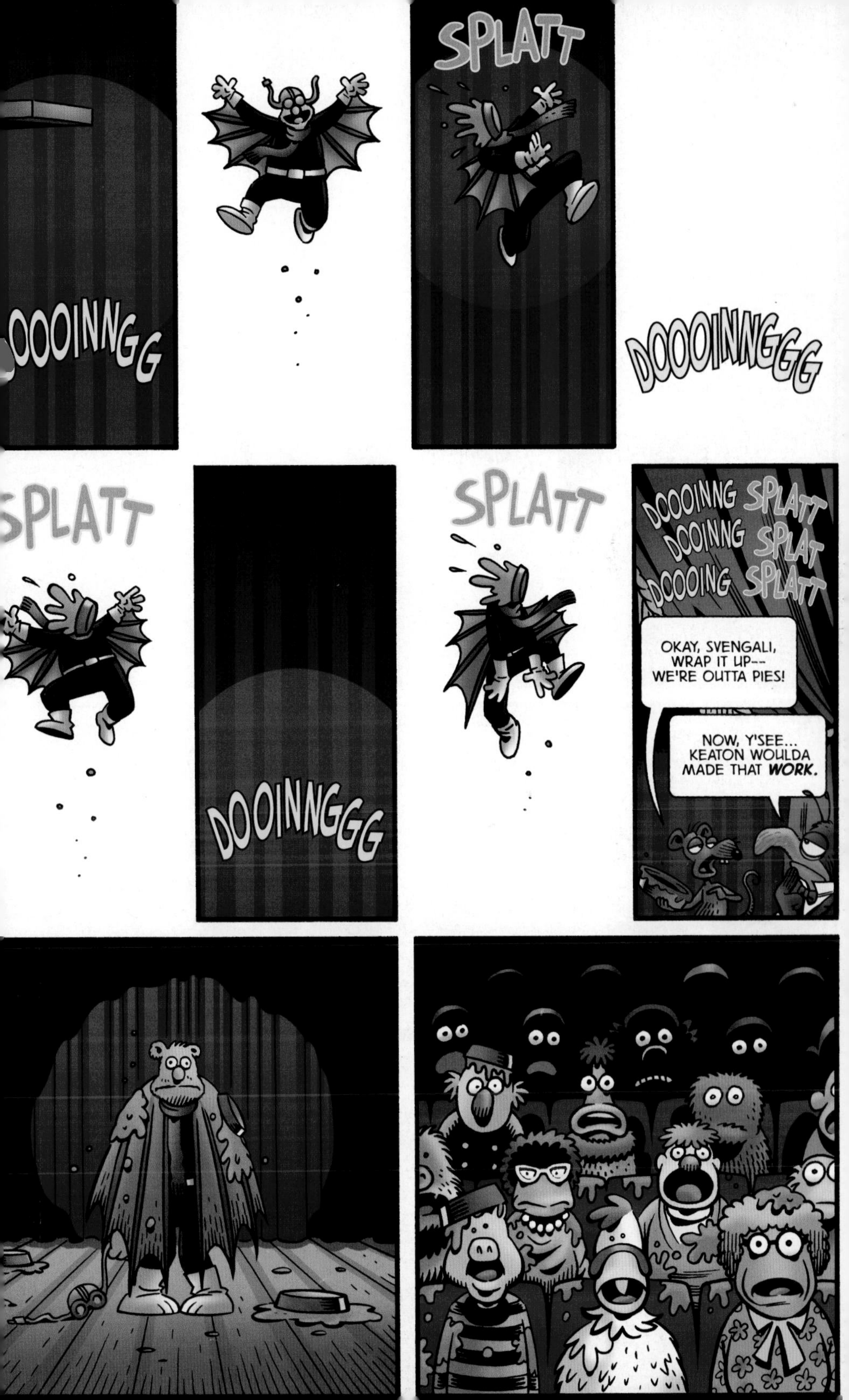
DOOOINNGG
SPLATT
DOOOINNGGG
SPLATT
DOOINNGGG
SPLATT
DOOOINNG SPLATT
DOOINNG SPLAT
DOOOING SPLATT
OKAY, SVENGALI, WRAP IT UP-- WE'RE OUTTA PIES!
NOW, Y'SEE... KEATON WOULDA MADE THAT WORK.

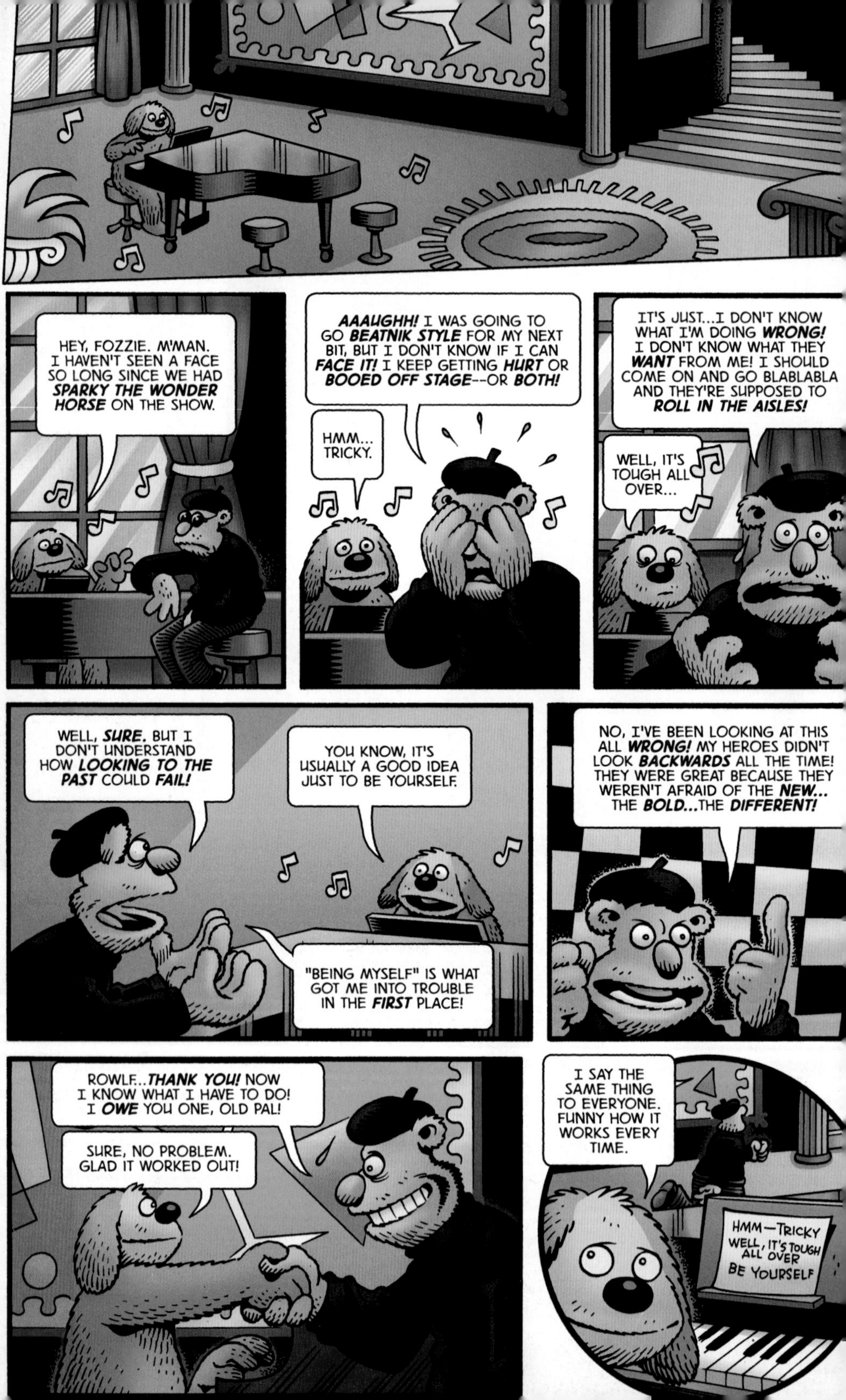
HEY, FOZZIE. M'MAN. I HAVEN'T SEEN A FACE SO LONG SINCE WE HAD SPARKY THE WONDER HORSE ON THE SHOW.
AAAUGHH! I WAS GOING TO GO BEATNIK STYLE FOR MY NEXT BIT, BUT I DON'T KNOW IF I CAN FACE IT! I KEEP GETTING HURT OR BOOED OFF STAGE--OR BOTH!
HMM... TRICKY.
IT'S JUST...I DON'T KNOW WHAT I'M DOING WRONG! I DON'T KNOW WHAT THEY WANT FROM ME! I SHOULD COME ON AND GO BLABLABLA AND THEY'RE SUPPOSED TO ROLL IN THE AISLES!
WELL, IT'S TOUGH ALL OVER...
WELL, SURE. BUT I DON'T UNDERSTAND HOW LOOKING TO THE PAST COULD FAIL!
YOU KNOW, IT'S USUALLY A GOOD IDEA JUST TO BE YOURSELF.
"BEING MYSELF" IS WHAT GOT ME INTO TROUBLE IN THE FIRST PLACE!
NO, I'VE BEEN LOOKING AT THIS ALL WRONG! MY HEROES DIDN'T LOOK BACKWARDS ALL THE TIME! THEY WERE GREAT BECAUSE THEY WEREN'T AFRAID OF THE NEW... THE BOLD...THE DIFFERENT!
ROWLF...THANK YOU! NOW I KNOW WHAT I HAVE TO DO! I OWE YOU ONE, OLD PAL!
SURE, NO PROBLEM. GLAD IT WORKED OUT!
I SAY THE SAME THING TO EVERYONE. FUNNY HOW IT WORKS EVERY TIME.
HMM—TRICKY
WELL, IT'S TOUGH ALL OVER
BE YOURSELF

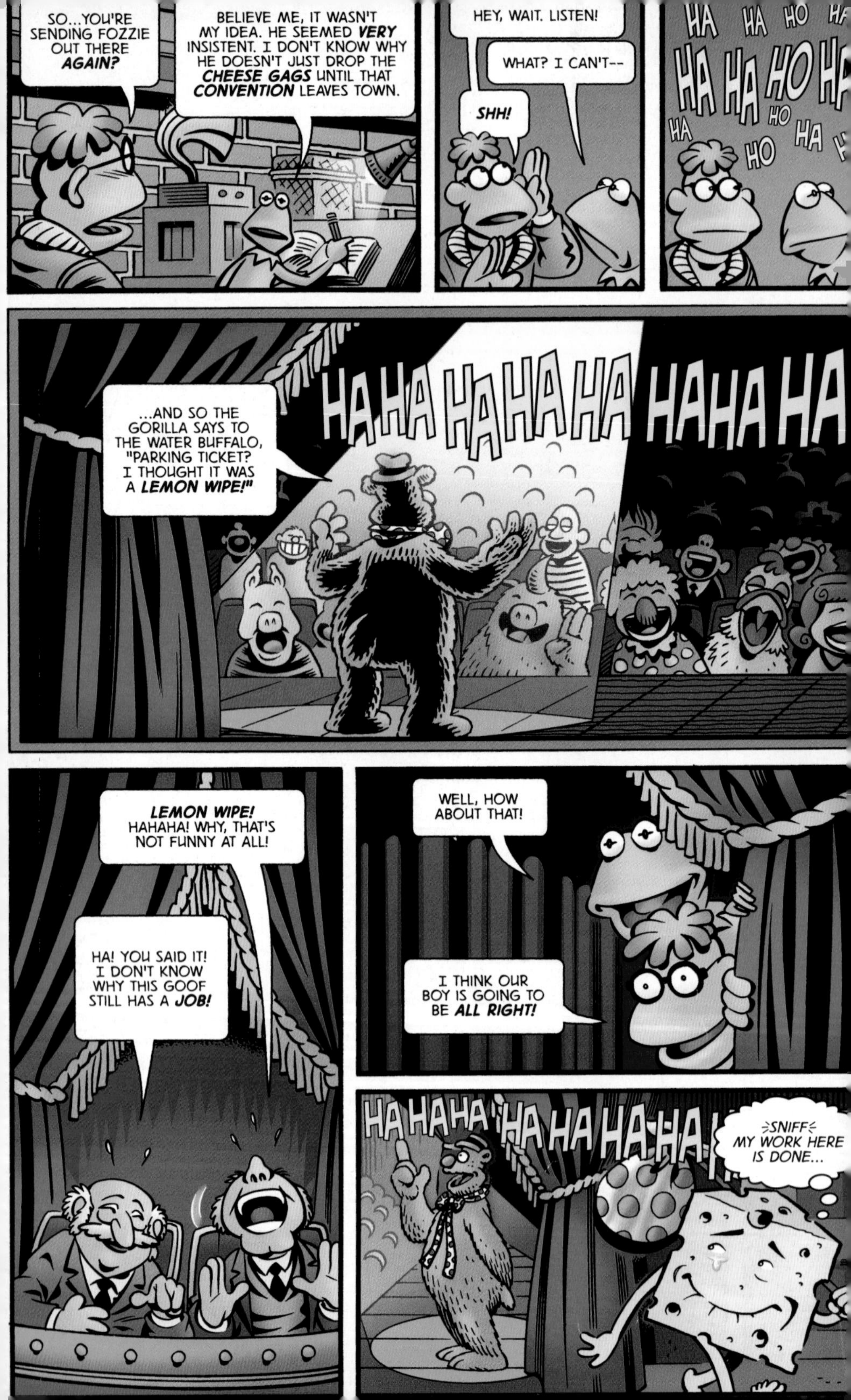

SO...YOU'RE SENDING FOZZIE OUT THERE *AGAIN?*
BELIEVE ME, IT WASN'T MY IDEA. HE SEEMED *VERY* INSISTENT. I DON'T KNOW WHY HE DOESN'T JUST DROP THE *CHEESE GAGS* UNTIL THAT *CONVENTION* LEAVES TOWN.
HEY, WAIT. LISTEN!
WHAT? I CAN'T--
SHH!
HA HA HO HA HA HA HO HA HA HO HO HA HA
...AND SO THE GORILLA SAYS TO THE WATER BUFFALO, "PARKING TICKET? I THOUGHT IT WAS A *LEMON WIPE!*"
HAHA HAHAHA HAHA HA
LEMON WIPE! HAHAHA! WHY, THAT'S NOT FUNNY AT ALL!
HA! YOU SAID IT! I DON'T KNOW WHY THIS GOOF STILL HAS A *JOB!*
WELL, HOW ABOUT THAT!
I THINK OUR BOY IS GOING TO BE *ALL RIGHT!*
HA HAHA HA HA HA HA HA
SNIFF MY WORK HERE IS DONE...

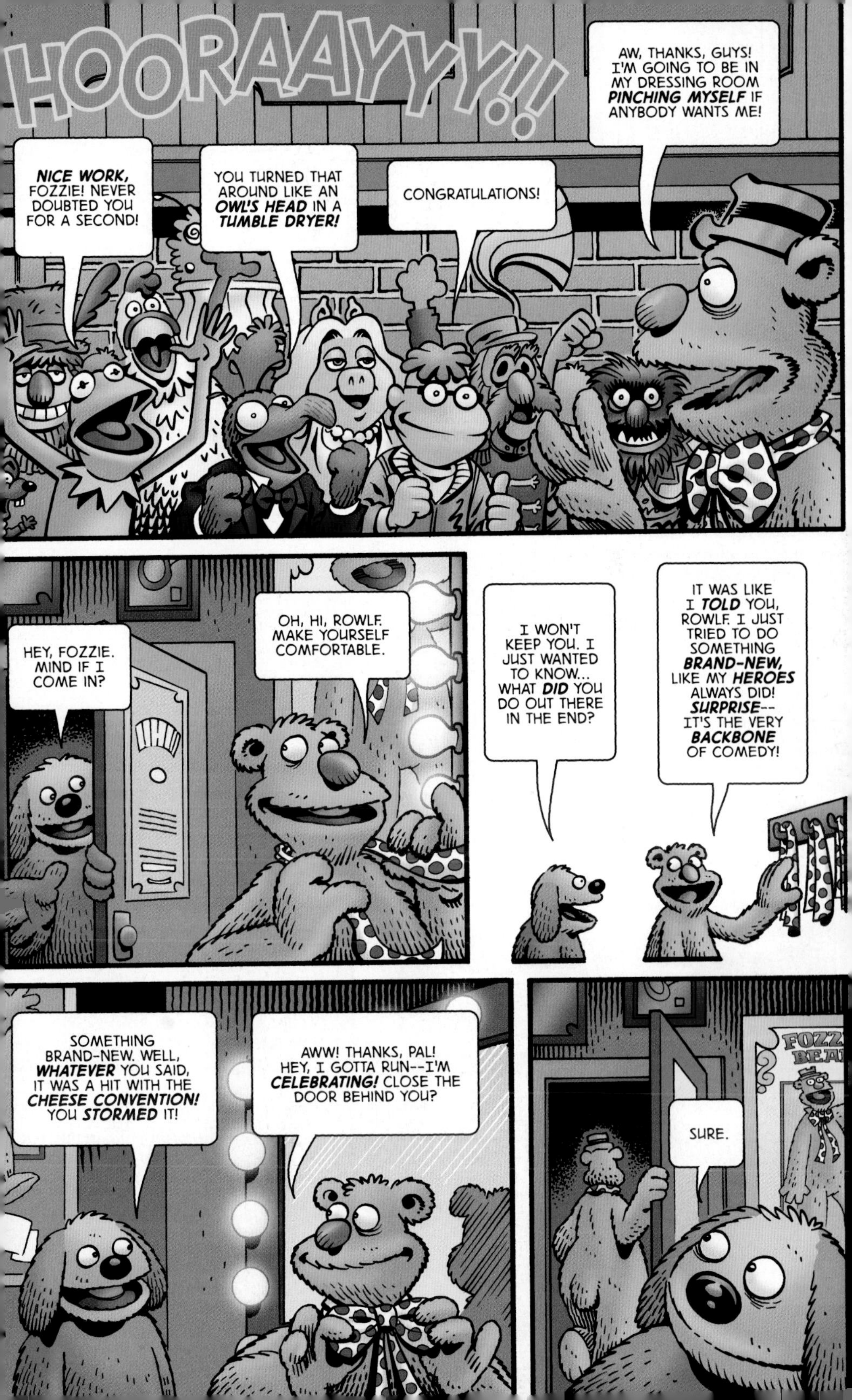
HOORAAYYY!!
AW, THANKS, GUYS! I'M GOING TO BE IN MY DRESSING ROOM PINCHING MYSELF IF ANYBODY WANTS ME!
NICE WORK, FOZZIE! NEVER DOUBTED YOU FOR A SECOND!
YOU TURNED THAT AROUND LIKE AN OWL'S HEAD IN A TUMBLE DRYER!
CONGRATULATIONS!
HEY, FOZZIE. MIND IF I COME IN?
OH, HI, ROWLF. MAKE YOURSELF COMFORTABLE.
I WON'T KEEP YOU. I JUST WANTED TO KNOW... WHAT DID YOU DO OUT THERE IN THE END?
IT WAS LIKE I TOLD YOU, ROWLF. I JUST TRIED TO DO SOMETHING BRAND-NEW, LIKE MY HEROES ALWAYS DID! SURPRISE-- IT'S THE VERY BACKBONE OF COMEDY!
SOMETHING BRAND-NEW. WELL, WHATEVER YOU SAID, IT WAS A HIT WITH THE CHEESE CONVENTION! YOU STORMED IT!
AWW! THANKS, PAL! HEY, I GOTTA RUN--I'M CELEBRATING! CLOSE THE DOOR BEHIND YOU?
SURE.

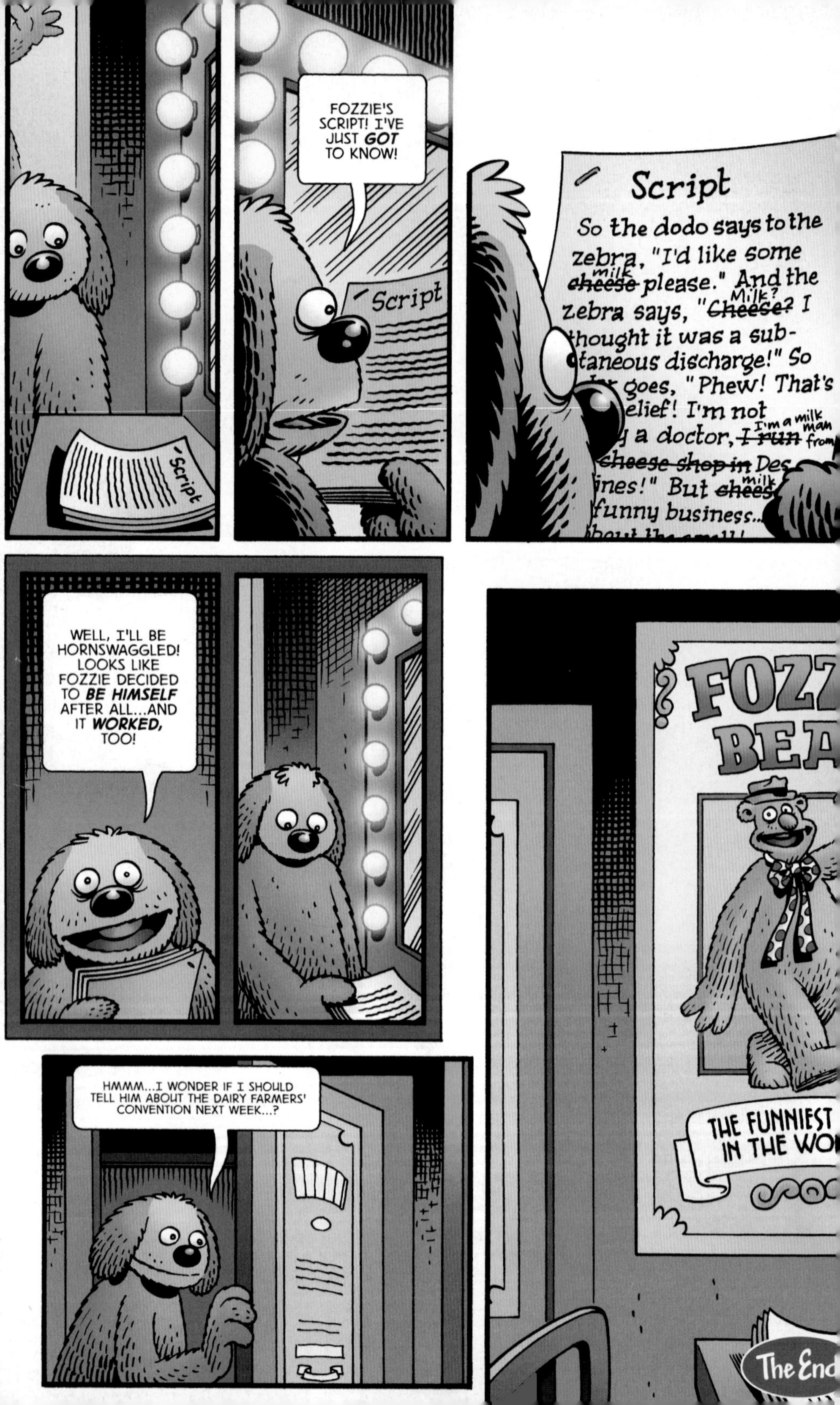

Script
FOZZIE'S SCRIPT! I'VE JUST **GOT** TO KNOW!
Script
So the dodo says to the zebra, "I'd like some ~~cheese~~ milk please." And the zebra says, "~~Cheese?~~ Milk? I thought it was a sub-taneous discharge!" So
goes, "Phew! That's
elief! I'm not
a doctor, ~~I run~~ I'm a milk man from
~~cheese shop in~~ Des
ines!" But ~~chees~~ milk
funny business...
WELL, I'LL BE HORNSWAGGLED! LOOKS LIKE FOZZIE DECIDED TO **BE HIMSELF** AFTER ALL...AND IT **WORKED,** TOO!
HMMM...I WONDER IF I SHOULD TELL HIM ABOUT THE DAIRY FARMERS' CONVENTION NEXT WEEK...?
FOZZ
BEA
THE FUNNIEST
IN THE WO
The End

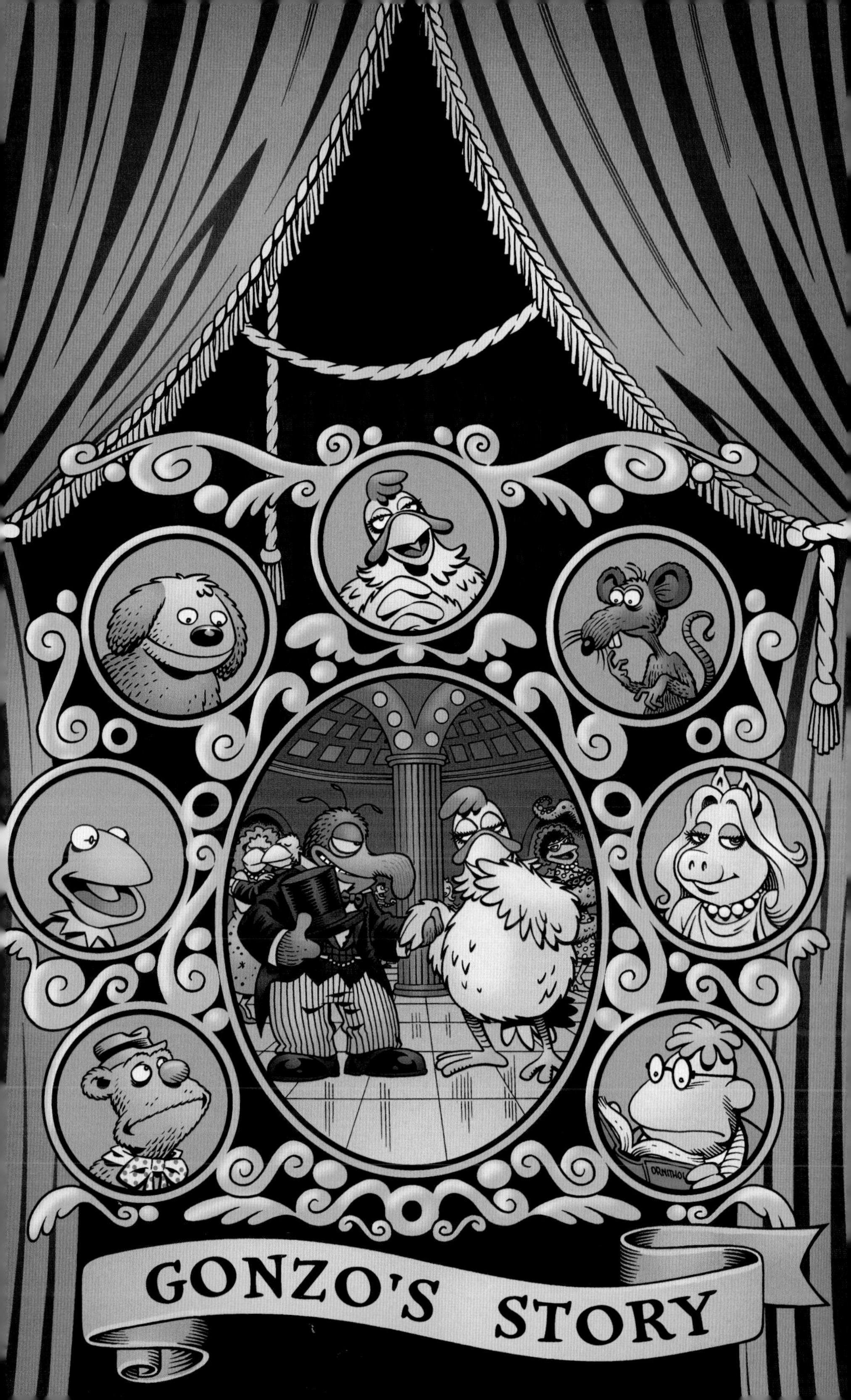
ORNITHOL
GONZO'S STORY

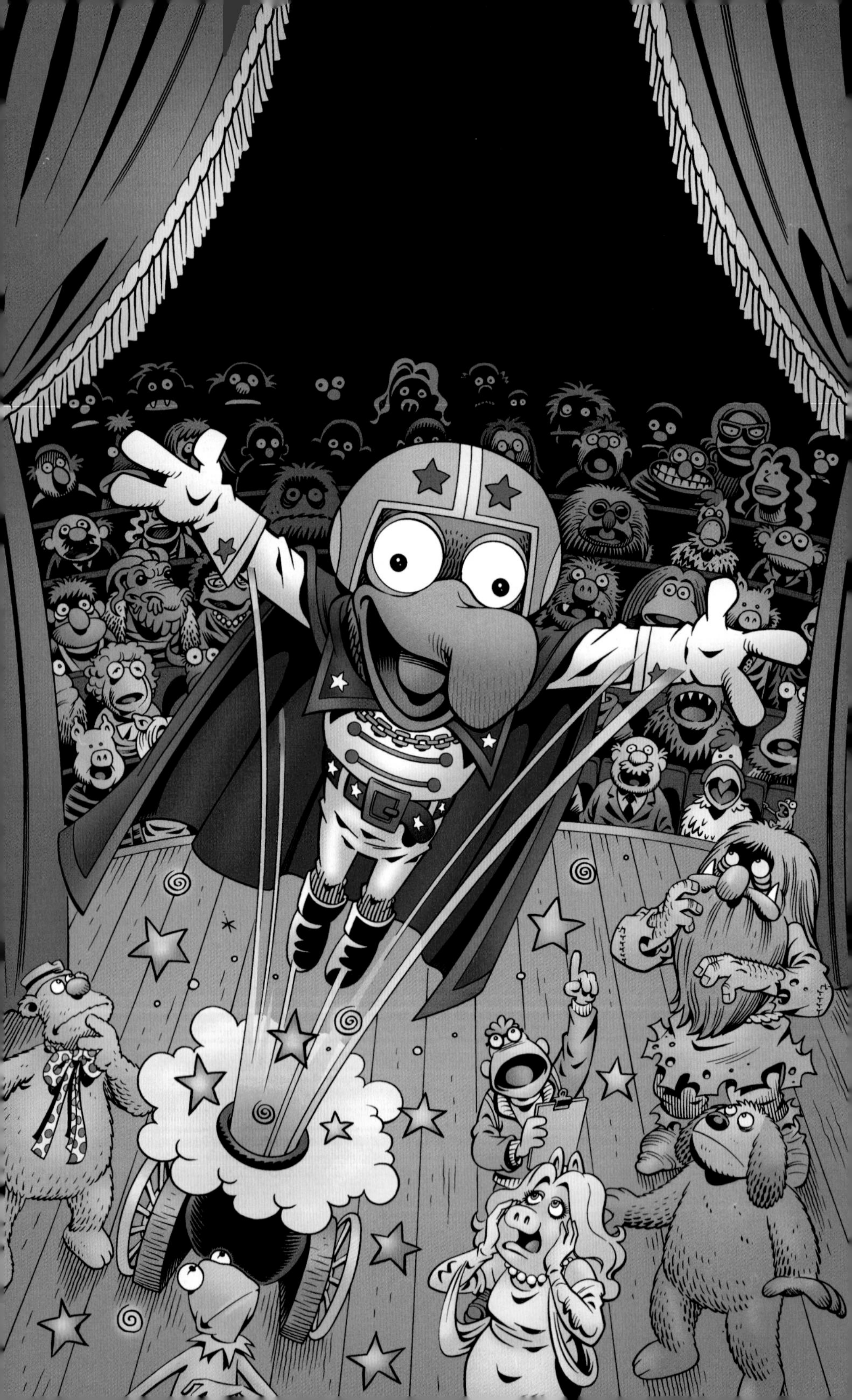

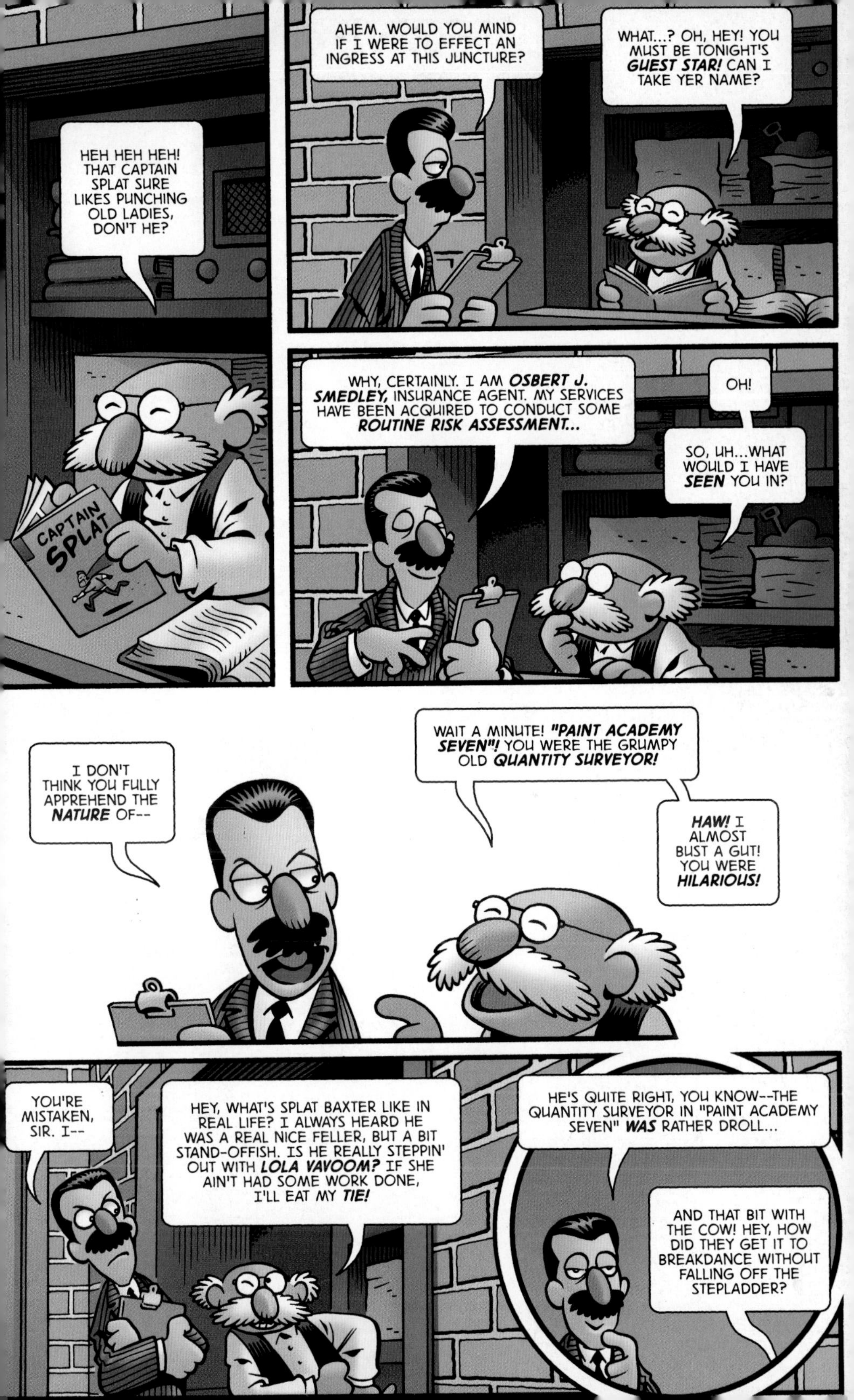
HEH HEH HEH! THAT CAPTAIN SPLAT SURE LIKES PUNCHING OLD LADIES, DON'T HE?
CAPTAIN SPLAT
AHEM. WOULD YOU MIND IF I WERE TO EFFECT AN INGRESS AT THIS JUNCTURE?
WHAT...? OH, HEY! YOU MUST BE TONIGHT'S GUEST STAR! CAN I TAKE YER NAME?
WHY, CERTAINLY. I AM OSBERT J. SMEDLEY, INSURANCE AGENT. MY SERVICES HAVE BEEN ACQUIRED TO CONDUCT SOME ROUTINE RISK ASSESSMENT...
OH!
SO, UH...WHAT WOULD I HAVE SEEN YOU IN?
WAIT A MINUTE! "PAINT ACADEMY SEVEN"! YOU WERE THE GRUMPY OLD QUANTITY SURVEYOR!
I DON'T THINK YOU FULLY APPREHEND THE NATURE OF--
HAW! I ALMOST BUST A GUT! YOU WERE HILARIOUS!
YOU'RE MISTAKEN, SIR. I--
HEY, WHAT'S SPLAT BAXTER LIKE IN REAL LIFE? I ALWAYS HEARD HE WAS A REAL NICE FELLER, BUT A BIT STAND-OFFISH. IS HE REALLY STEPPIN' OUT WITH LOLA VAVOOM? IF SHE AIN'T HAD SOME WORK DONE, I'LL EAT MY TIE!
HE'S QUITE RIGHT, YOU KNOW--THE QUANTITY SURVEYOR IN "PAINT ACADEMY SEVEN" WAS RATHER DROLL...
AND THAT BIT WITH THE COW! HEY, HOW DID THEY GET IT TO BREAKDANCE WITHOUT FALLING OFF THE STEPLADDER?

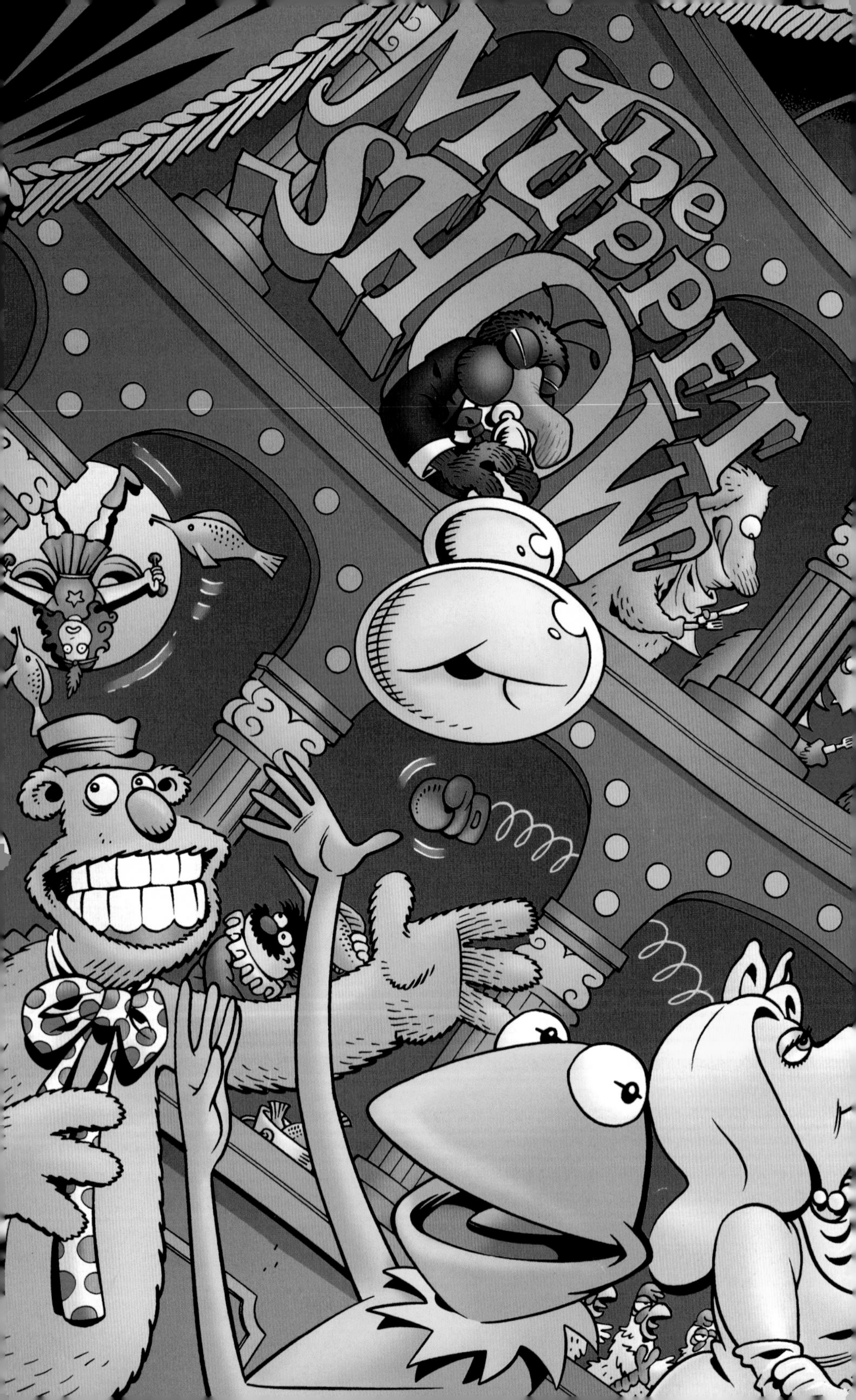
The Muppet Show

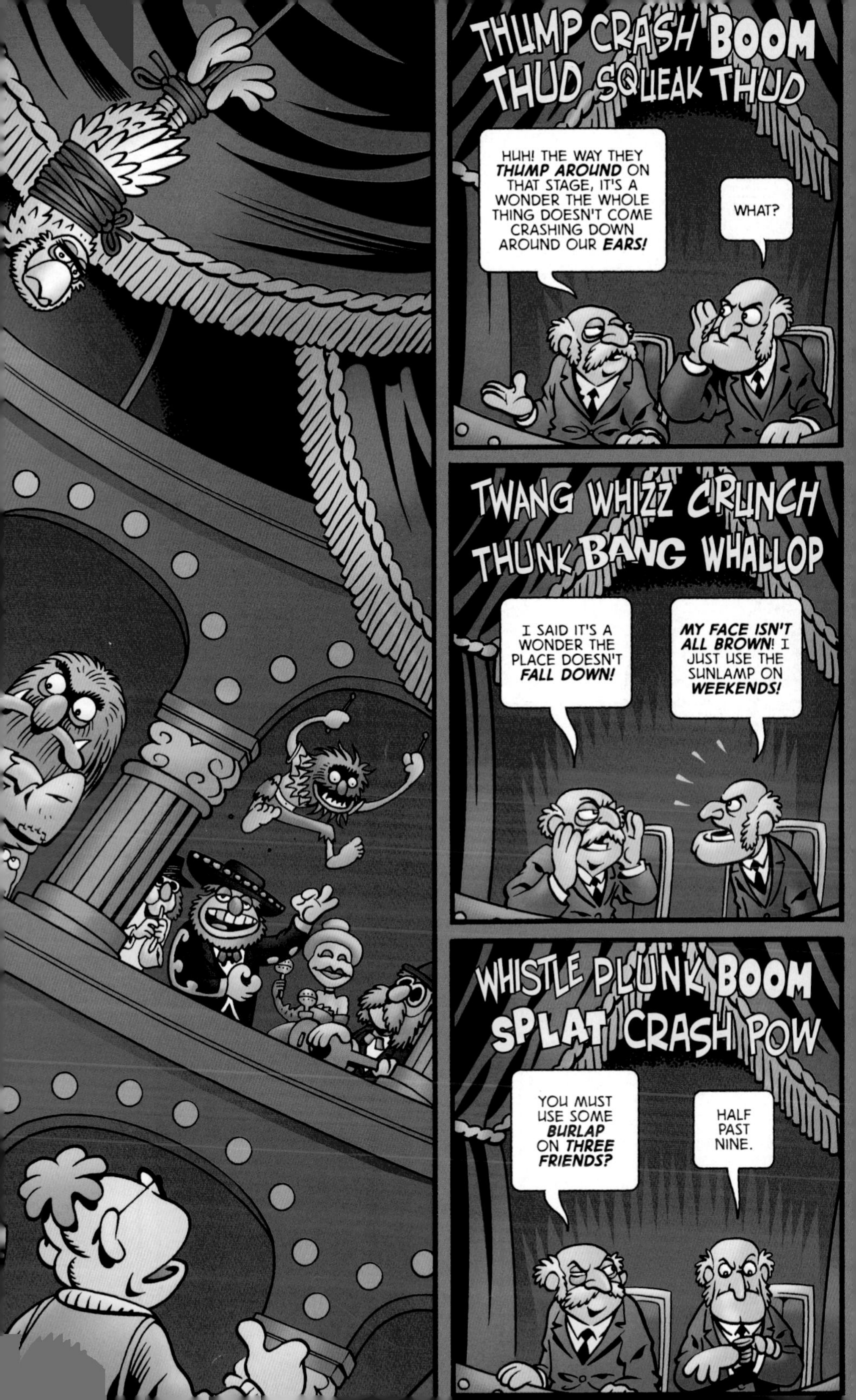
THUMP CRASH BOOM
THUD SQUEAK THUD
HUH! THE WAY THEY *THUMP AROUND* ON THAT STAGE, IT'S A WONDER THE WHOLE THING DOESN'T COME CRASHING DOWN AROUND OUR *EARS!*
WHAT?
TWANG WHIZZ CRUNCH
THUNK BANG WHALLOP
I SAID IT'S A WONDER THE PLACE DOESN'T *FALL DOWN!*
MY FACE ISN'T ALL BROWN! I JUST USE THE SUNLAMP ON *WEEKENDS!*
WHISTLE PLUNK BOOM
SPLAT CRASH POW
YOU MUST USE SOME *BURLAP* ON *THREE FRIENDS?*
HALF PAST NINE.

HMM...BACKSTAGE CLUTTER...FIRE HAZARD. I BELIEVE THAT'S **LEAD** PAINT.

ER, EXCUSE ME...? CAN I HELP YOU?

AH, YOU MUST BE MISTER THE FROG. **SMEDLEY'S** THE NAME. I'M FROM THE **CLAIM-YE-NOT INSURANCE COMPANY.** JUST A FEW ROUTINE QUESTIONS, IF YOU WOULDN'T MIND...

OH. WELL, I'M SURE **SCOOTER** CAN HELP YOU...

HEY, SCOOTER--TELL MISTER SMEDLEY WHAT HE WANTS TO KNOW, WILL YOU? I'VE GOT TO GET THESE BOOKS TO BALANCE BY FRIDAY.

SURE THING, BOSS.

EXCELLENT. NOW, FOR MEDICAL INSURANCE PURPOSES, I NEED TO KNOW WHAT **SPECIES** EVERYBODY IS.

OH, SURE, THAT'S **EASY.** WE'VE GOT HUMANS, COWS, PIGS, FROGS, BEARS, DOGS, RATS...

...EAGLES, SHEEP, LOBSTERS, KING PRAWNS...THERE'S A GORILLA, BUT HE'S UNDER A TEMPORARY CONTRACT...

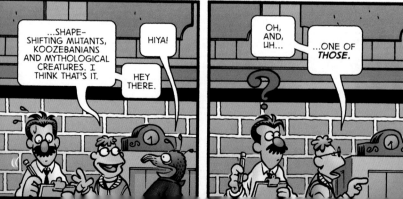

...SHAPE-SHIFTING MUTANTS, KOOZEBANIANS AND MYTHOLOGICAL CREATURES. I THINK THAT'S IT.

HIYA!

HEY THERE.

OH, AND, UH...

...ONE OF **THOSE.**

NEXT:

CULTURE!

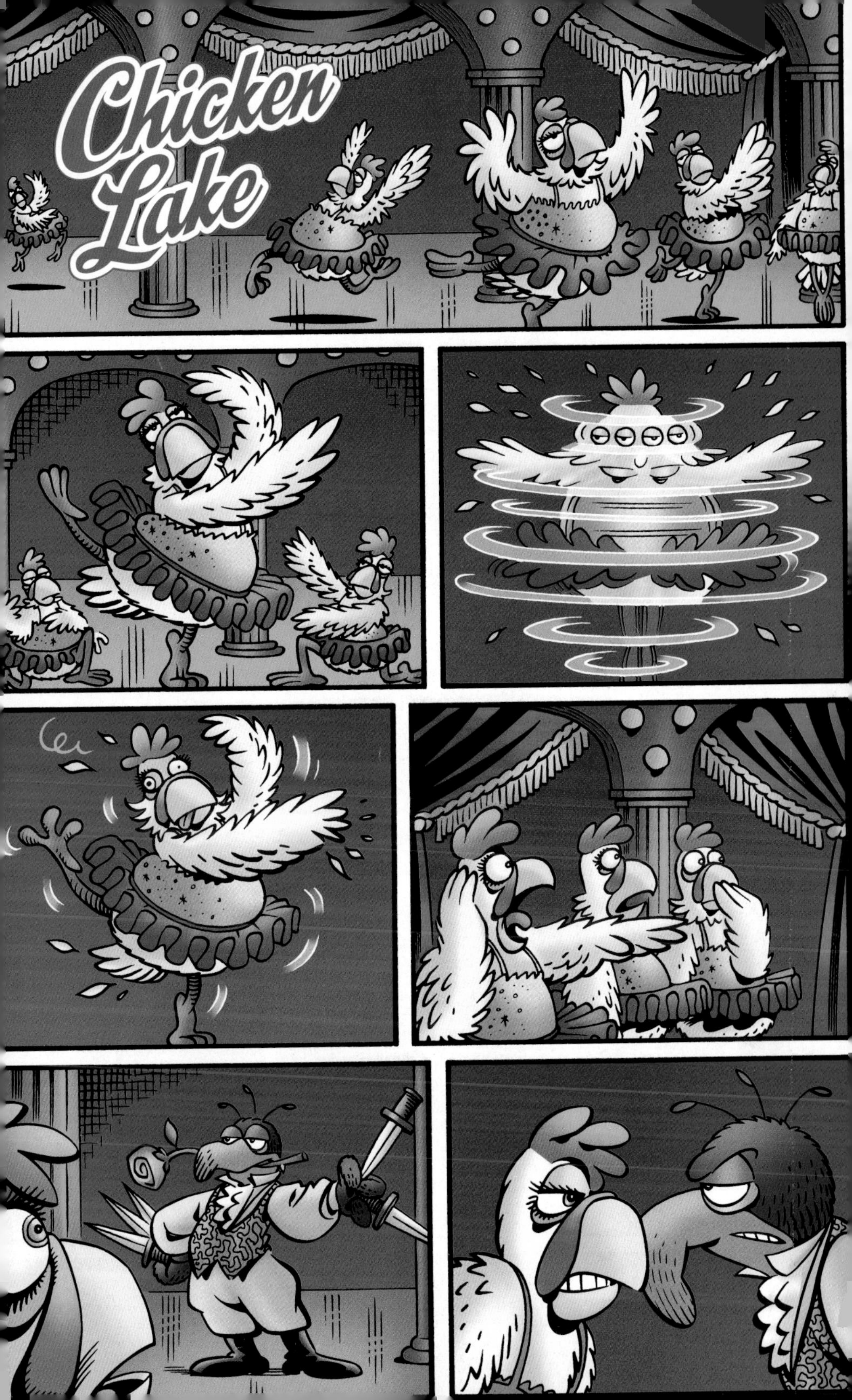
Chicken Lake

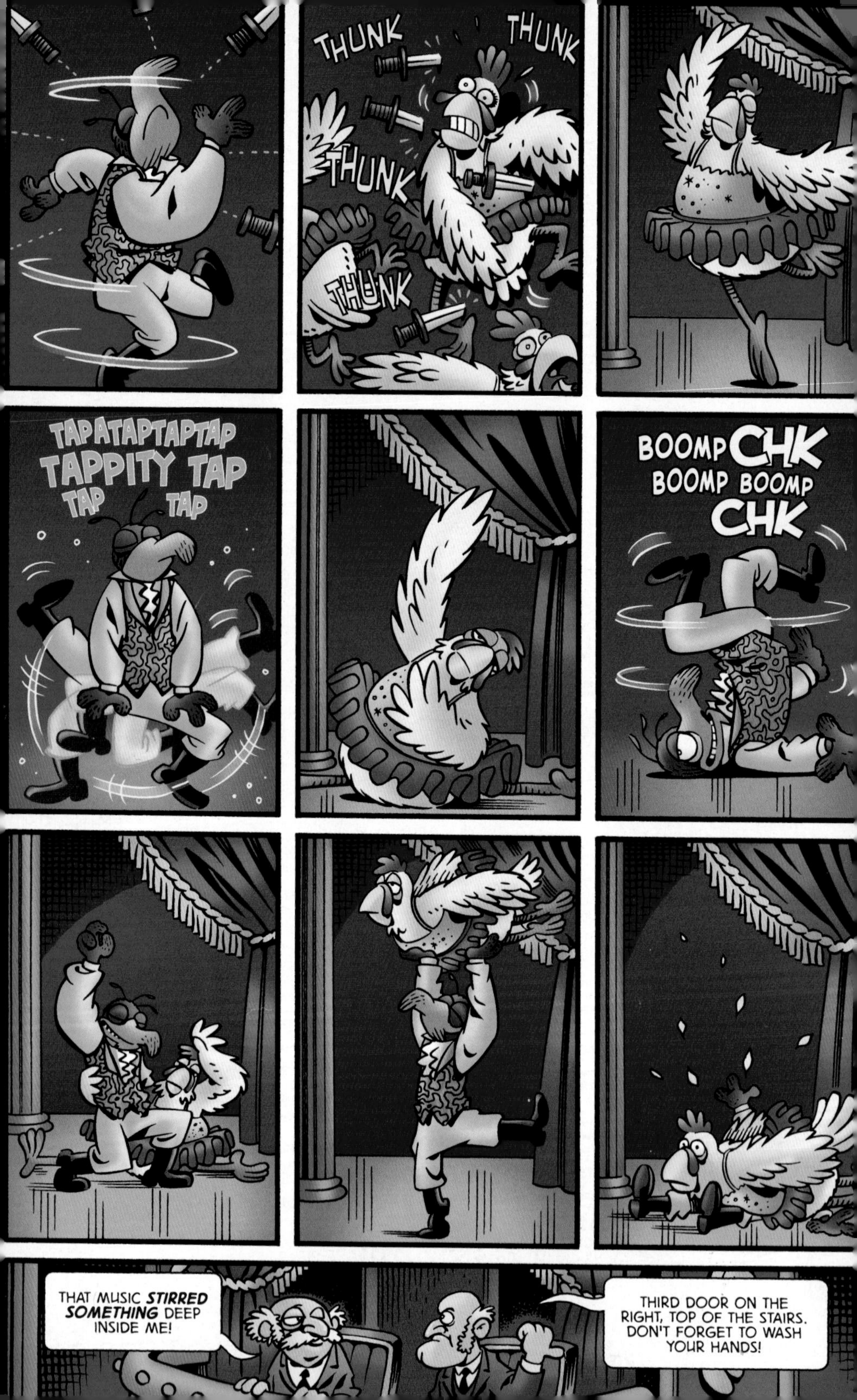
THUNK
THUNK
THUNK
THUNK
TAPATAPTAPTAPTAP
TAPPITY TAP
TAP
TAP
BOOMP CHK
BOOMP BOOMP
CHK
THAT MUSIC STIRRED SOMETHING DEEP INSIDE ME!
THIRD DOOR ON THE RIGHT, TOP OF THE STAIRS. DON'T FORGET TO WASH YOUR HANDS!

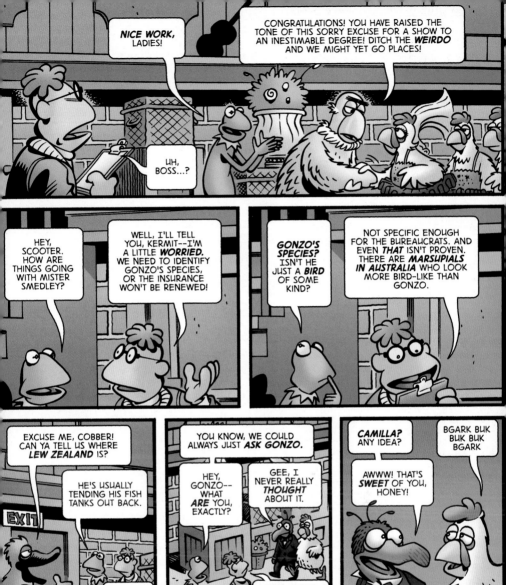

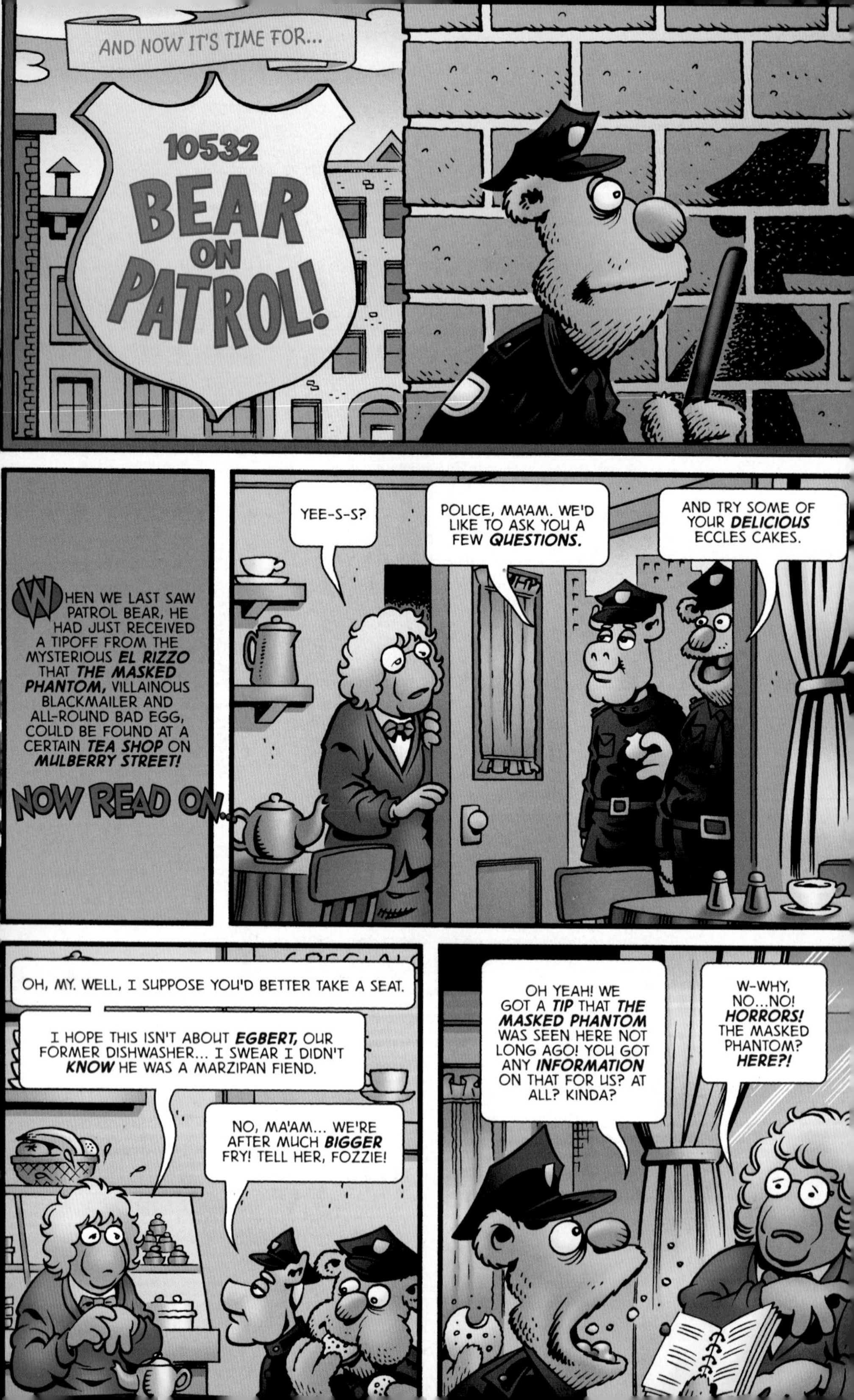

AND NOW IT'S TIME FOR...
10532
BEAR ON PATROL!
WHEN WE LAST SAW PATROL BEAR, HE HAD JUST RECEIVED A TIPOFF FROM THE MYSTERIOUS EL RIZZO THAT THE MASKED PHANTOM, VILLAINOUS BLACKMAILER AND ALL-ROUND BAD EGG, COULD BE FOUND AT A CERTAIN TEA SHOP ON MULBERRY STREET!
NOW READ ON...
YEE-S-S?
POLICE, MA'AM. WE'D LIKE TO ASK YOU A FEW QUESTIONS.
AND TRY SOME OF YOUR DELICIOUS ECCLES CAKES.
OH, MY. WELL, I SUPPOSE YOU'D BETTER TAKE A SEAT.
I HOPE THIS ISN'T ABOUT EGBERT, OUR FORMER DISHWASHER... I SWEAR I DIDN'T KNOW HE WAS A MARZIPAN FIEND.
NO, MA'AM... WE'RE AFTER MUCH BIGGER FRY! TELL HER, FOZZIE!
OH YEAH! WE GOT A TIP THAT THE MASKED PHANTOM WAS SEEN HERE NOT LONG AGO! YOU GOT ANY INFORMATION ON THAT FOR US? AT ALL? KINDA?
W-WHY, NO...NO! HORRORS! THE MASKED PHANTOM? HERE?!

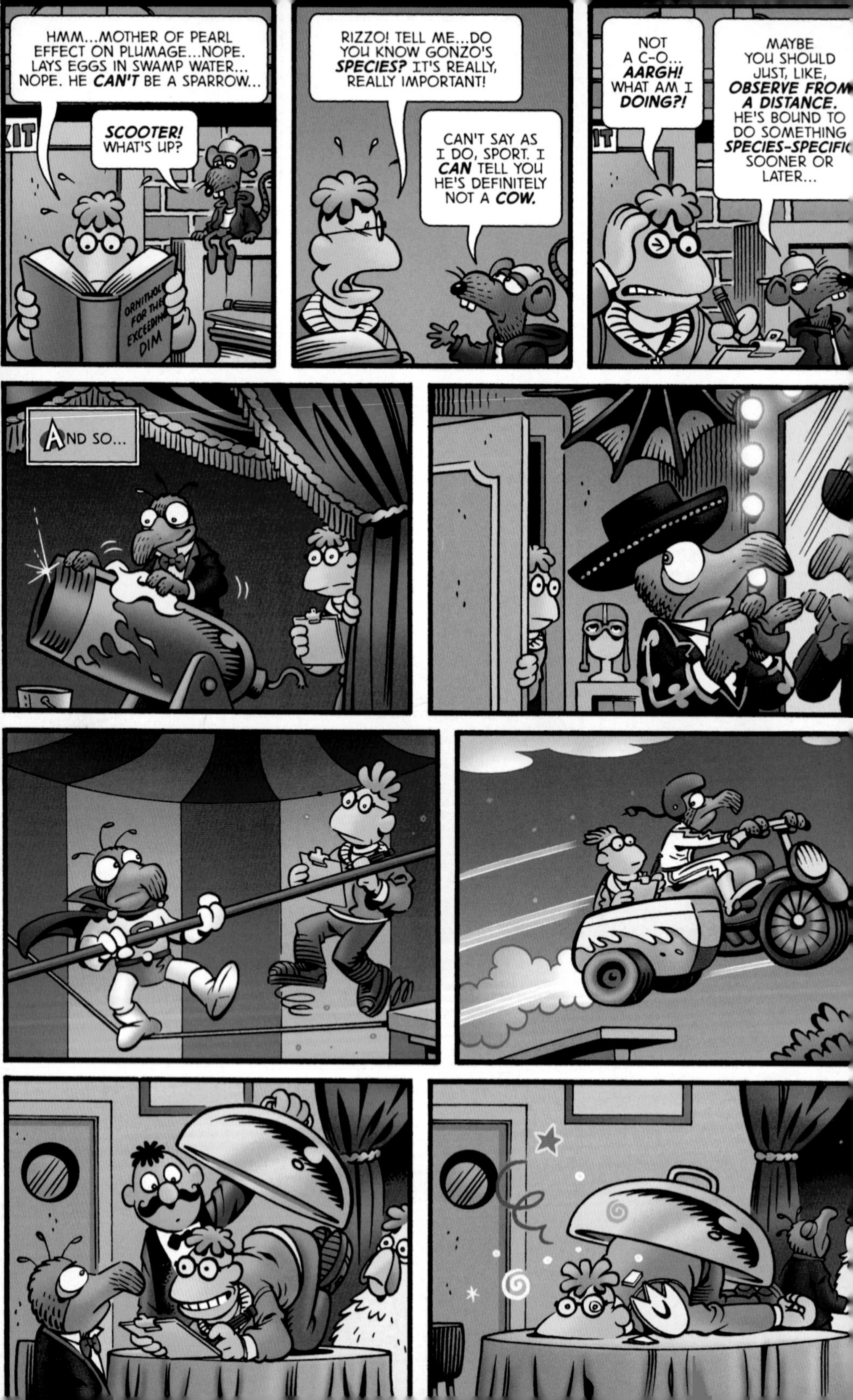
HMM...MOTHER OF PEARL EFFECT ON PLUMAGE...NOPE. LAYS EGGS IN SWAMP WATER... NOPE. HE CAN'T BE A SPARROW...
SCOOTER! WHAT'S UP?
ORNITHOLO FOR THE EXCEEDIN DIM
RIZZO! TELL ME...DO YOU KNOW GONZO'S SPECIES? IT'S REALLY, REALLY IMPORTANT!
CAN'T SAY AS I DO, SPORT. I CAN TELL YOU HE'S DEFINITELY NOT A COW.
NOT A C-O... AARGH! WHAT AM I DOING?!
MAYBE YOU SHOULD JUST, LIKE, OBSERVE FROM A DISTANCE. HE'S BOUND TO DO SOMETHING SPECIES-SPECIFIC SOONER OR LATER...
AND SO...

OKAY...THIS DOESN'T ADD UP AT *ALL*.

HE *CAN'T* BE A DODO. I'M MISSING SOMETHING FUNDAMENTAL... BUT WHAT? *WHAT??*

CRESTED GRE~~
~~DUSKY WARBLER~~
~~LESSER-SPOTTED~~

DODO
OSTRICH
PUKEKO
??

TIME TO TRY A *DIFFERENT TACK!* MAYBE I CAN APPROACH THIS BY *CONSENSUS!*

~~W~~HAT DO *YOU* THINK GONZO IS?

I ALWAYS THOUGHT HE WAS SOME KIND OF *ANTEATER.*

CLEARLY THE RESULT OF *SCIENCE GONE MAD!*

NOT THAT WE SCIENTISTS *GO* MAD, YOU UNDERSTAND.

HOÉR BÜRK DER ÜMLÄÜT ÜRN DER BØËKY-BØËK?

LOB-STER! LOB-STER! *AAAAHHH!*

MAN, HE CAN SWING *ANY* WHICH WAY...I CAN DIG IT.

I, FOR ONE, WOULD LIKE TO THINK OF HIM AS AN *HOMME TRÉS* GENTLE.

UNFORTUNATELY, HE'S TOO *WEIRD.*

MEEP! MEEP MEEP MEEP MEEP *MEEP!*

GONZO? IS HE THE GREEN FELLER WITH THE FLIPPERS OR THE HAIRY ONE IN THE HAT?

>SIGH<

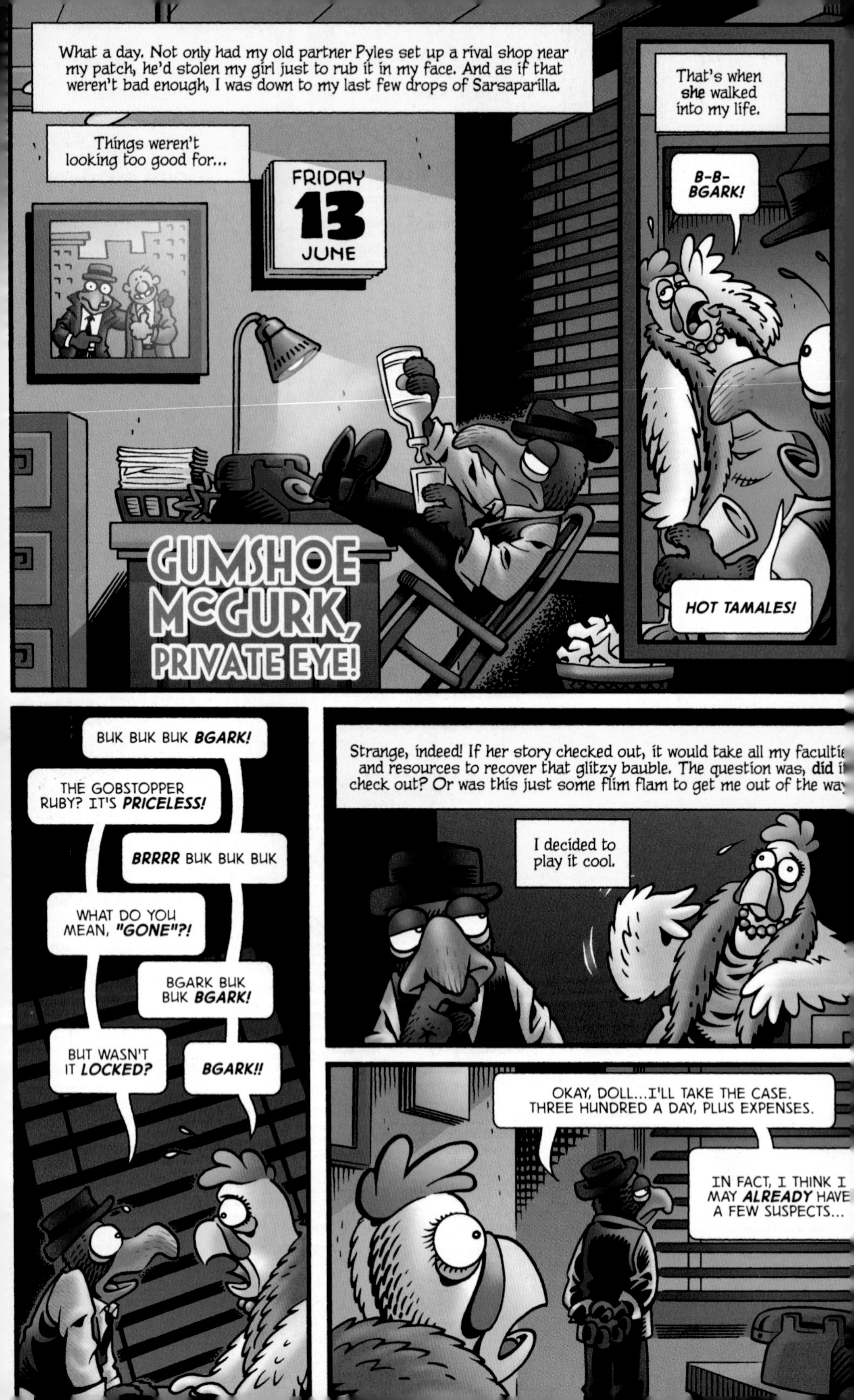
What a day. Not only had my old partner Pyles set up a rival shop near my patch, he'd stolen my girl just to rub it in my face. And as if that weren't bad enough, I was down to my last few drops of Sarsaparilla.
Things weren't looking too good for...
FRIDAY 13 JUNE
GUMSHOE McGURK, PRIVATE EYE!
That's when she walked into my life.
B-B-BGARK!
HOT TAMALES!
BUK BUK BUK BGARK!
THE GOBSTOPPER RUBY? IT'S PRICELESS!
BRRRR BUK BUK BUK
WHAT DO YOU MEAN, "GONE"?!
BGARK BUK BUK BGARK!
BUT WASN'T IT LOCKED?
BGARK!!
Strange, indeed! If her story checked out, it would take all my facultie and resources to recover that glitzy bauble. The question was, did i check out? Or was this just some flim flam to get me out of the way
I decided to play it cool.
OKAY, DOLL...I'LL TAKE THE CASE. THREE HUNDRED A DAY, PLUS EXPENSES.
IN FACT, I THINK I MAY ALREADY HAVE A FEW SUSPECTS...

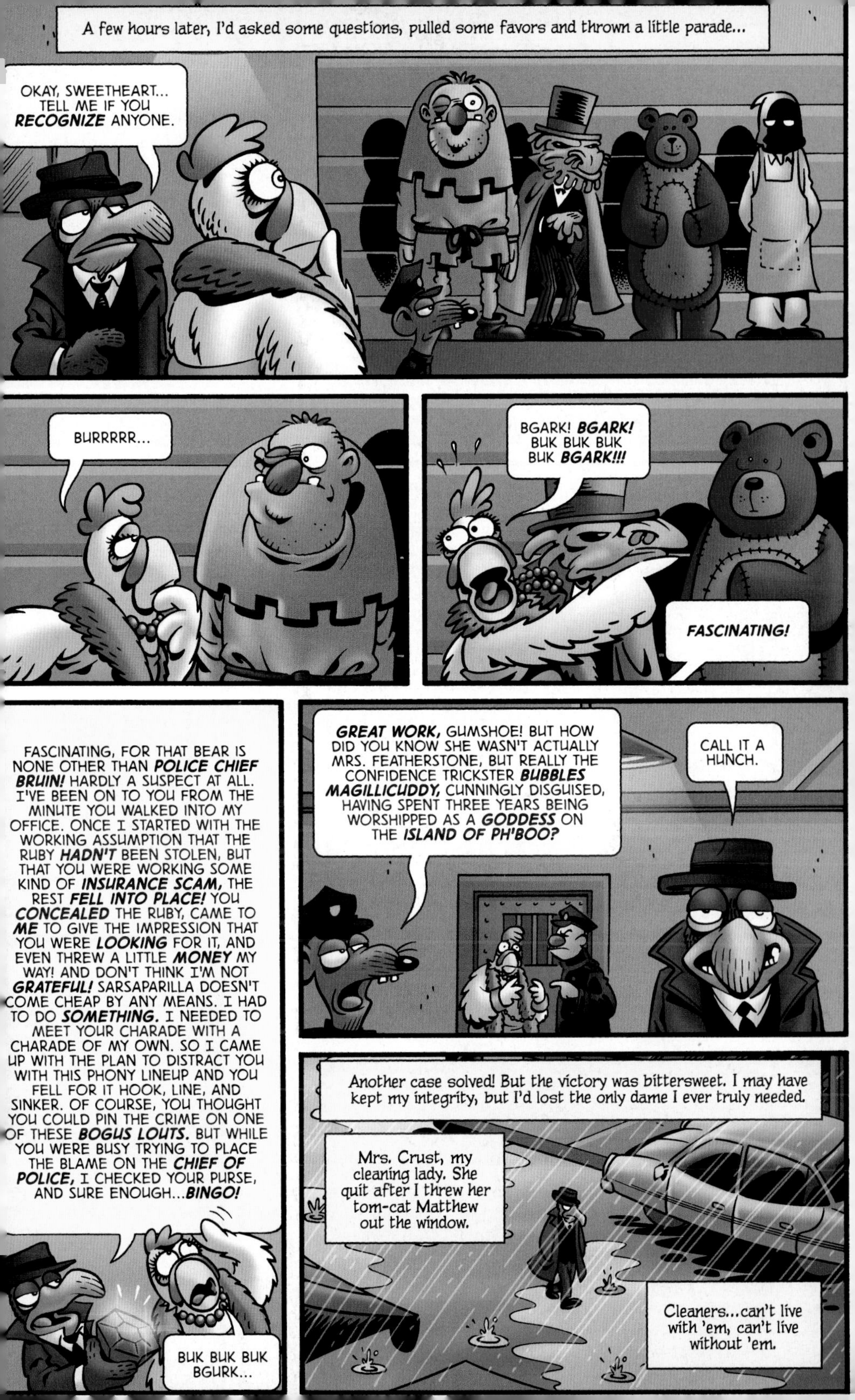
A few hours later, I'd asked some questions, pulled some favors and thrown a little parade...
OKAY, SWEETHEART... TELL ME IF YOU RECOGNIZE ANYONE.
BURRRRR...
BGARK! BGARK! BUK BUK BUK BUK BGARK!!!
FASCINATING!
FASCINATING, FOR THAT BEAR IS NONE OTHER THAN POLICE CHIEF BRUIN! HARDLY A SUSPECT AT ALL. I'VE BEEN ON TO YOU FROM THE MINUTE YOU WALKED INTO MY OFFICE. ONCE I STARTED WITH THE WORKING ASSUMPTION THAT THE RUBY HADN'T BEEN STOLEN, BUT THAT YOU WERE WORKING SOME KIND OF INSURANCE SCAM, THE REST FELL INTO PLACE! YOU CONCEALED THE RUBY, CAME TO ME TO GIVE THE IMPRESSION THAT YOU WERE LOOKING FOR IT, AND EVEN THREW A LITTLE MONEY MY WAY! AND DON'T THINK I'M NOT GRATEFUL! SARSAPARILLA DOESN'T COME CHEAP BY ANY MEANS. I HAD TO DO SOMETHING. I NEEDED TO MEET YOUR CHARADE WITH A CHARADE OF MY OWN. SO I CAME UP WITH THE PLAN TO DISTRACT YOU WITH THIS PHONY LINEUP AND YOU FELL FOR IT HOOK, LINE, AND SINKER. OF COURSE, YOU THOUGHT YOU COULD PIN THE CRIME ON ONE OF THESE BOGUS LOUTS. BUT WHILE YOU WERE BUSY TRYING TO PLACE THE BLAME ON THE CHIEF OF POLICE, I CHECKED YOUR PURSE, AND SURE ENOUGH...BINGO!
BUK BUK BUK BGURK...
GREAT WORK, GUMSHOE! BUT HOW DID YOU KNOW SHE WASN'T ACTUALLY MRS. FEATHERSTONE, BUT REALLY THE CONFIDENCE TRICKSTER BUBBLES MAGILLICUDDY, CUNNINGLY DISGUISED, HAVING SPENT THREE YEARS BEING WORSHIPPED AS A GODDESS ON THE ISLAND OF PH'BOO?
CALL IT A HUNCH.
Another case solved! But the victory was bittersweet. I may have kept my integrity, but I'd lost the only dame I ever truly needed.
Mrs. Crust, my cleaning lady. She quit after I threw her tom-cat Matthew out the window.
Cleaners...can't live with 'em, can't live without 'em.

PIGS in SPACE!

And now it's time for...

Starring

CAPTAIN LINK HOGTHROB

FIRST MATE MISS PIGGY

And the supercilious DR STRANGEPORK!

WHEN WE LAST SAW THE GOOD SHIP **SWINETREK**, IT HAD BEEN CHARGED WITH BRINGING A **STRANGE, UNIDENTIFIED SHIP** TO THE INTERGALACTIC AUTHORITIES! **NOW READ ON.**

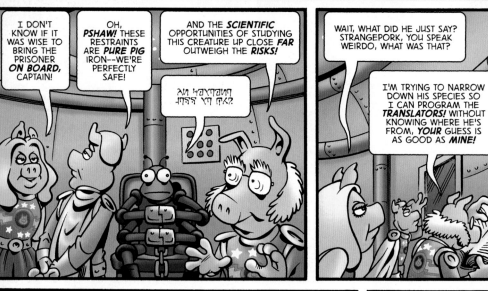

I DON'T KNOW IF IT WAS WISE TO BRING THE PRISONER **ON BOARD**, CAPTAIN!

OH, **PSHAW!** THESE RESTRAINTS ARE **PURE PIG** IRON--WE'RE PERFECTLY SAFE!

AND THE **SCIENTIFIC** OPPORTUNITIES OF STUDYING THIS CREATURE UP CLOSE **FAR** OUTWEIGH THE **RISKS!**

WAIT, WHAT DID HE JUST SAY? STRANGEPORK, YOU SPEAK WEIRDO, WHAT WAS THAT?

I'M TRYING TO NARROW DOWN HIS SPECIES SO I CAN PROGRAM THE **TRANSLATORS!** WITHOUT KNOWING WHERE HE'S FROM, **YOUR** GUESS IS AS GOOD AS **MINE!**

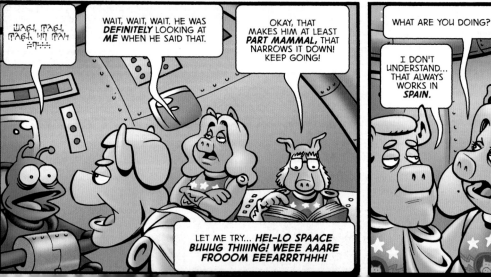

WAIT, WAIT, WAIT. HE WAS **DEFINITELY** LOOKING AT **ME** WHEN HE SAID THAT.

OKAY, THAT MAKES HIM AT LEAST **PART MAMMAL**, THAT NARROWS IT DOWN! KEEP GOING!

WHAT ARE YOU DOING?

I DON'T UNDERSTAND... THAT ALWAYS WORKS IN **SPAIN.**

LET ME TRY... **HEL-LO SPAACE BUUUG THIIIING! WEEE AAARE FROOOM EEEARRRTHHH!**

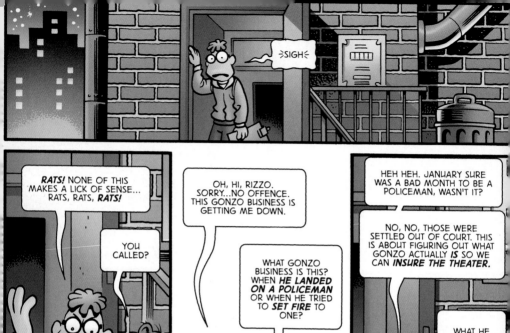

RATS! NONE OF THIS MAKES A LICK OF SENSE... RATS, RATS, **RATS!**

YOU CALLED?

OH, HI, RIZZO. SORRY...NO OFFENCE. THIS GONZO BUSINESS IS GETTING ME DOWN.

WHAT GONZO BUSINESS IS THIS? WHEN *HE LANDED ON A POLICEMAN* OR WHEN HE TRIED TO *SET FIRE* TO ONE?

HEH HEH. JANUARY SURE WAS A BAD MONTH TO BE A POLICEMAN, WASN'T IT?

NO, NO, THOSE WERE SETTLED OUT OF COURT. THIS IS ABOUT FIGURING OUT WHAT GONZO ACTUALLY *IS* SO WE CAN *INSURE THE THEATER.*

WHAT HE *IS?* ISN'T IT *OBVIOUS?*

IS IT?

SURE! HE'S A *GONZO... GONZO THE GREAT!* THE *ONE!* THE *ONLY!* THE *BEST!*

HE'S *UNIQUE,* SCOOTER! *UTTERLY* ONE-OF-A KIND!

YOU KNOW...I GUESS HE *IS!* HE MAY BE A SCRAWNY, HOMELY, UNCATEGORIZABLE *THING*...BUT HE'S *OUR* SCRAWNY, HOMELY, UNCATEGORIZABLE THING!

MISTER SMEDLEY... *YOU'VE GOT YOUR ANSWER!*

ATTABOY! AND I'M *100% BEHIND YA,* AS LONG AS YOU REMEMBER THAT IF IT GOES *WRONG* IT WAS *NOTHING TO DO WITH ME!*

NOW, IF YOU'LL EXCUSE ME, IT'S TIME FOR THE ALL-RODENT MARTIAL ARTS EXTRAVAGANZA THAT IS...

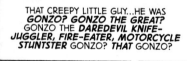

EXTRAVAGONZO!

HE FLIES THROUGH THE AIR WITH SUCH STYLE AND SUCH GRACE! HE'S GONZO THE GREAT AND HE'S HOT ON THE CASE! IT JUST TAKES A MOMENT TO SEE WHAT WE MEAN-- HE'S GONZO THE GREAT AND HE'S STEALING THE SCENE!

HE'S ALWAYS EXCITING, HE'S ALWAYS A THRILL! THAT GONZO KEEPS MOVING, HE NEVER STAYS STILL!

SO ROLL UP AND SEE HIM, HE'S TRYING AGAIN-- HE'S FLYING THROUGH SPACE AND DEFYING THE PAIN! HE'S READY TO DO IT, HE'S NOTHING TO LOSE-- HE'S CLIMBED IN THE CANNON, HE'S LIGHTING THE FUSE!

FROM CANNONS AND CATAPULTS, TRAPS AND BALLOONS, THAT GONZO COMES FLYING, TO POPULAR TUNES!

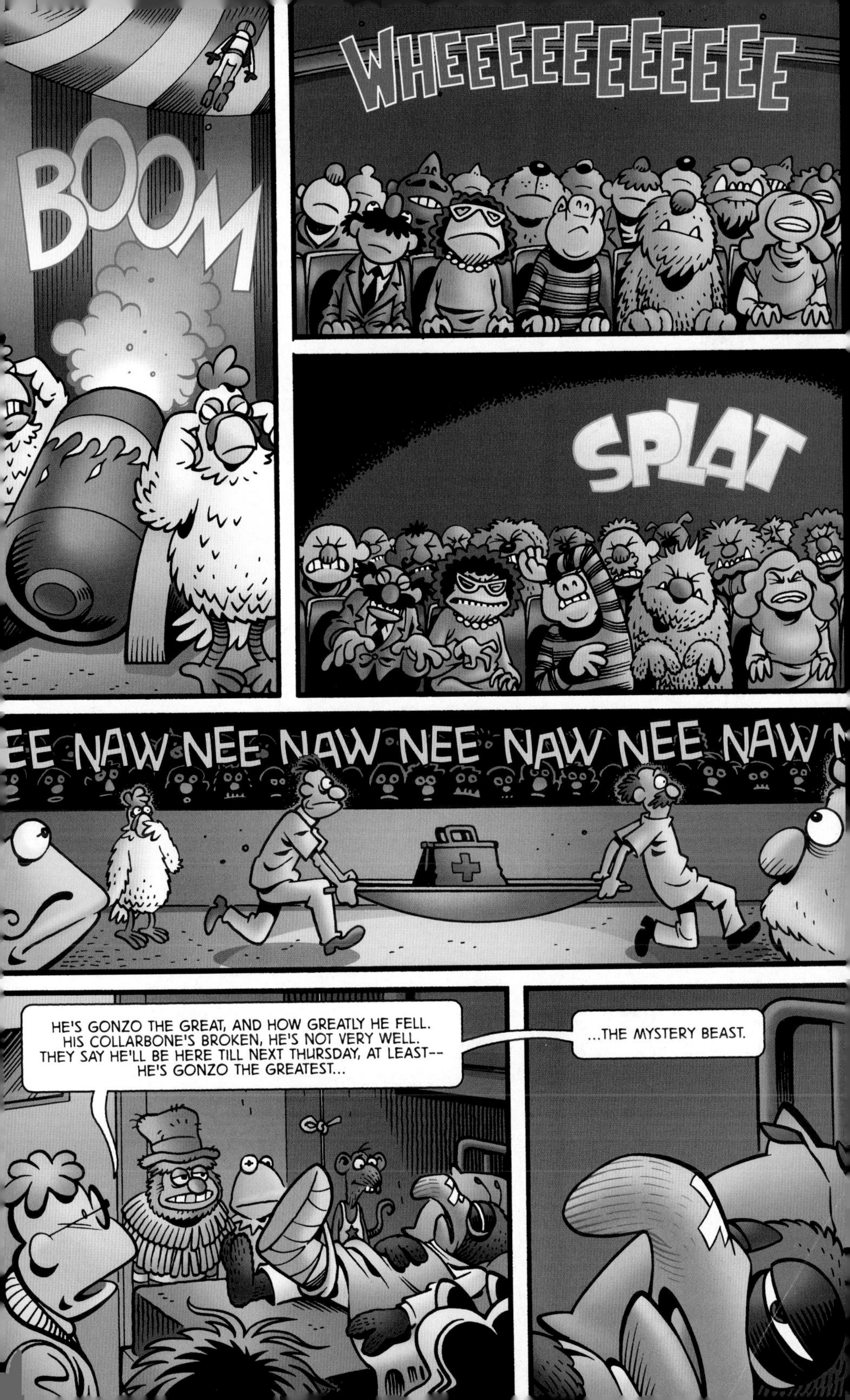
BOOM
WHEEEEEEEEEEEE
SPLAT
EE NAW NEE NAW NEE NAW NEE NAW
HE'S GONZO THE GREAT, AND HOW GREATLY HE FELL. HIS COLLARBONE'S BROKEN, HE'S NOT VERY WELL. THEY SAY HE'LL BE HERE TILL NEXT THURSDAY, AT LEAST-- HE'S GONZO THE GREATEST...
...THE MYSTERY BEAST.

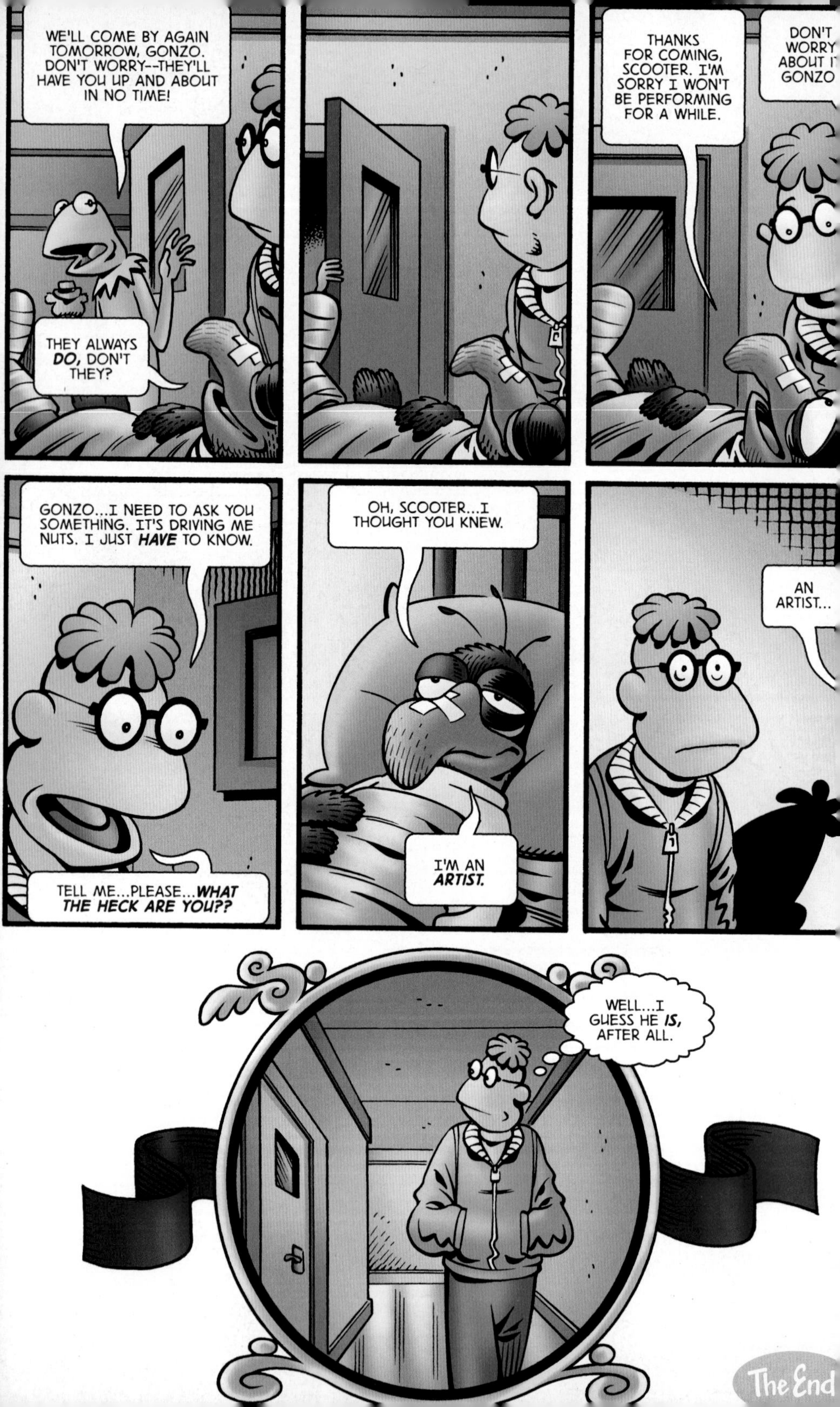
WE'LL COME BY AGAIN TOMORROW, GONZO. DON'T WORRY--THEY'LL HAVE YOU UP AND ABOUT IN NO TIME!
THEY ALWAYS *DO,* DON'T THEY?
THANKS FOR COMING, SCOOTER. I'M SORRY I WON'T BE PERFORMING FOR A WHILE.
DON'T WORRY ABOUT IT GONZO
GONZO...I NEED TO ASK YOU SOMETHING. IT'S DRIVING ME NUTS. I JUST *HAVE* TO KNOW.
TELL ME...PLEASE...*WHAT THE HECK ARE YOU??*
OH, SCOOTER...I THOUGHT YOU KNEW.
I'M AN *ARTIST.*
AN ARTIST...
WELL...I GUESS HE *IS,* AFTER ALL.
The End

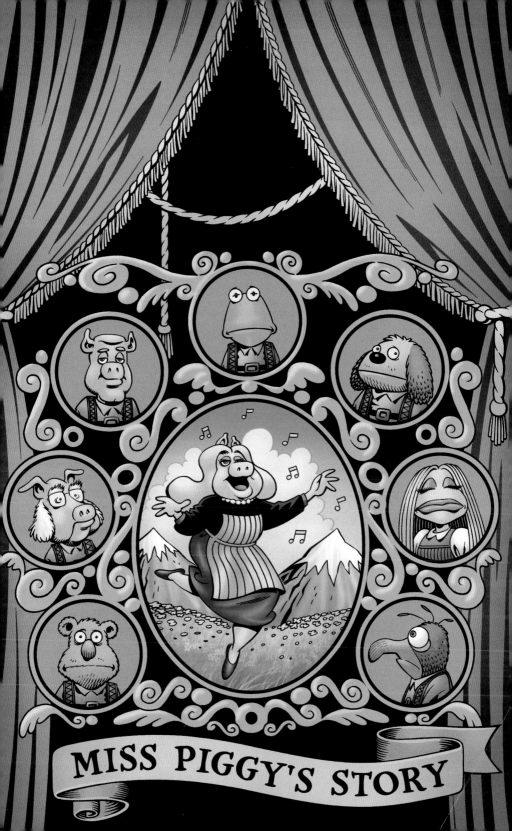

MISS PIGGY'S STORY

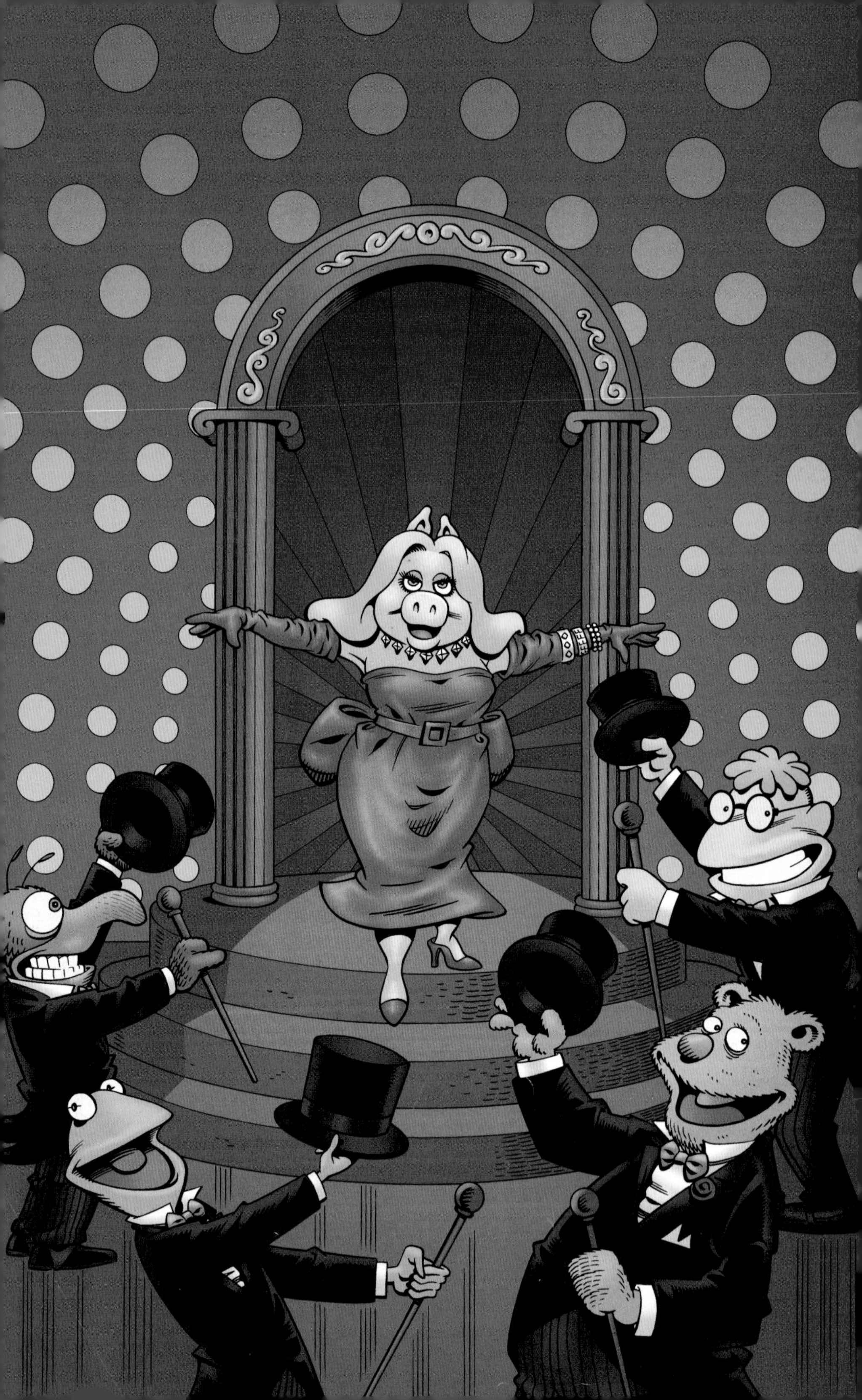

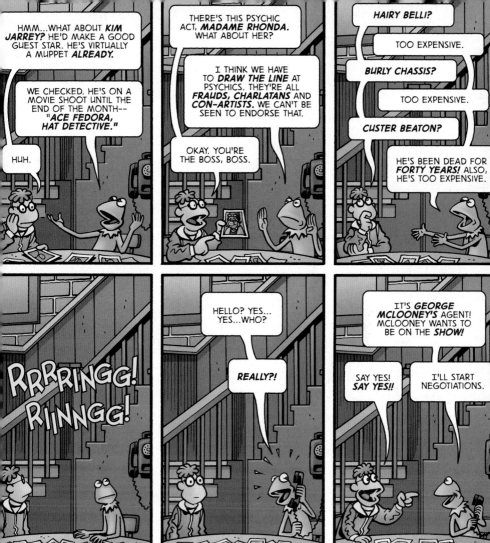
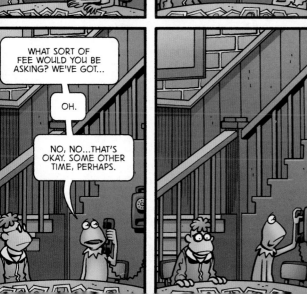

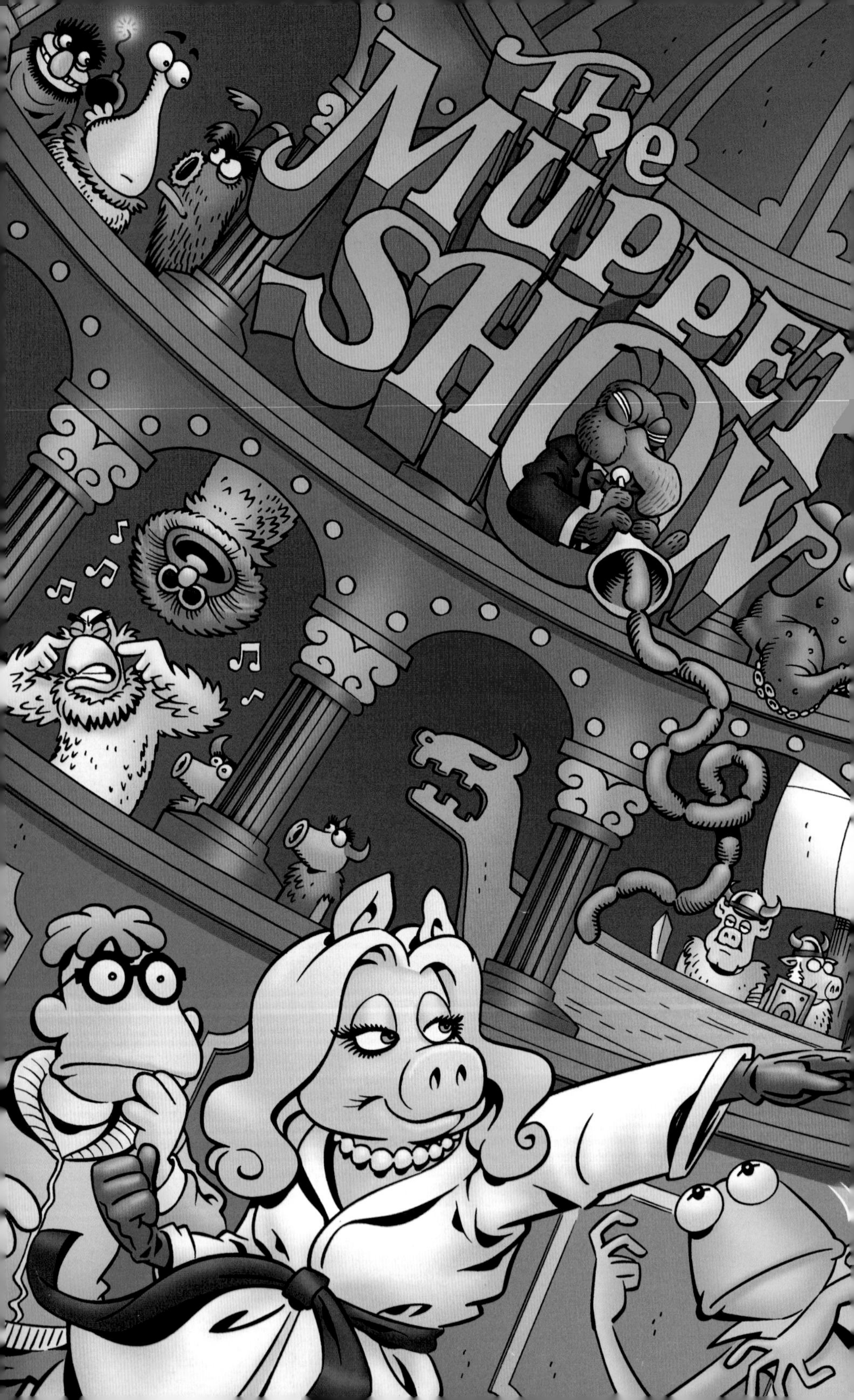
The Muppet Show

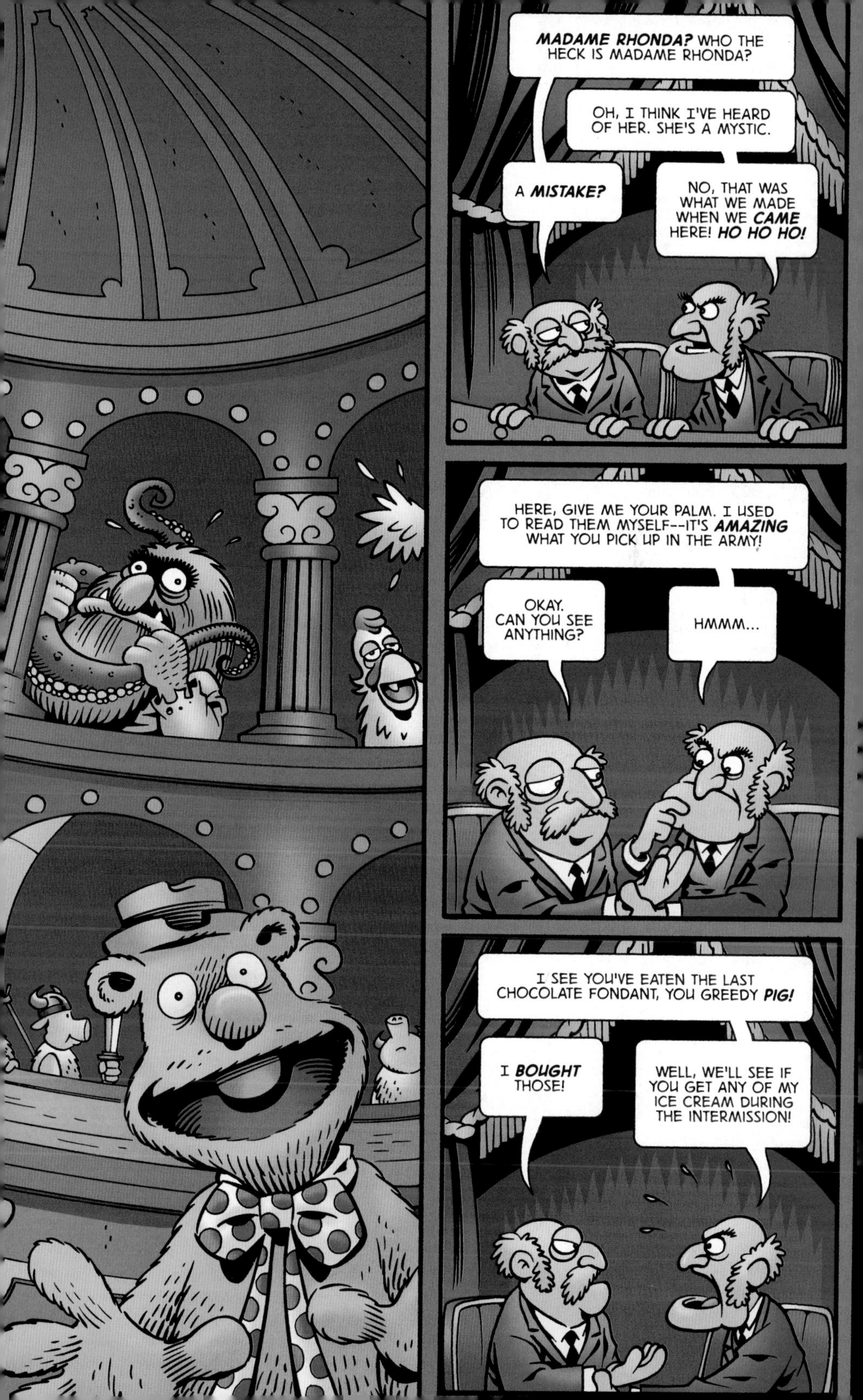
MADAME RHONDA? WHO THE HECK IS MADAME RHONDA?
OH, I THINK I'VE HEARD OF HER. SHE'S A MYSTIC.
A MISTAKE?
NO, THAT WAS WHAT WE MADE WHEN WE CAME HERE! HO HO HO!
HERE, GIVE ME YOUR PALM. I USED TO READ THEM MYSELF--IT'S AMAZING WHAT YOU PICK UP IN THE ARMY!
OKAY. CAN YOU SEE ANYTHING?
HMMM...
I SEE YOU'VE EATEN THE LAST CHOCOLATE FONDANT, YOU GREEDY PIG!
I BOUGHT THOSE!
WELL, WE'LL SEE IF YOU GET ANY OF MY ICE CREAM DURING THE INTERMISSION!

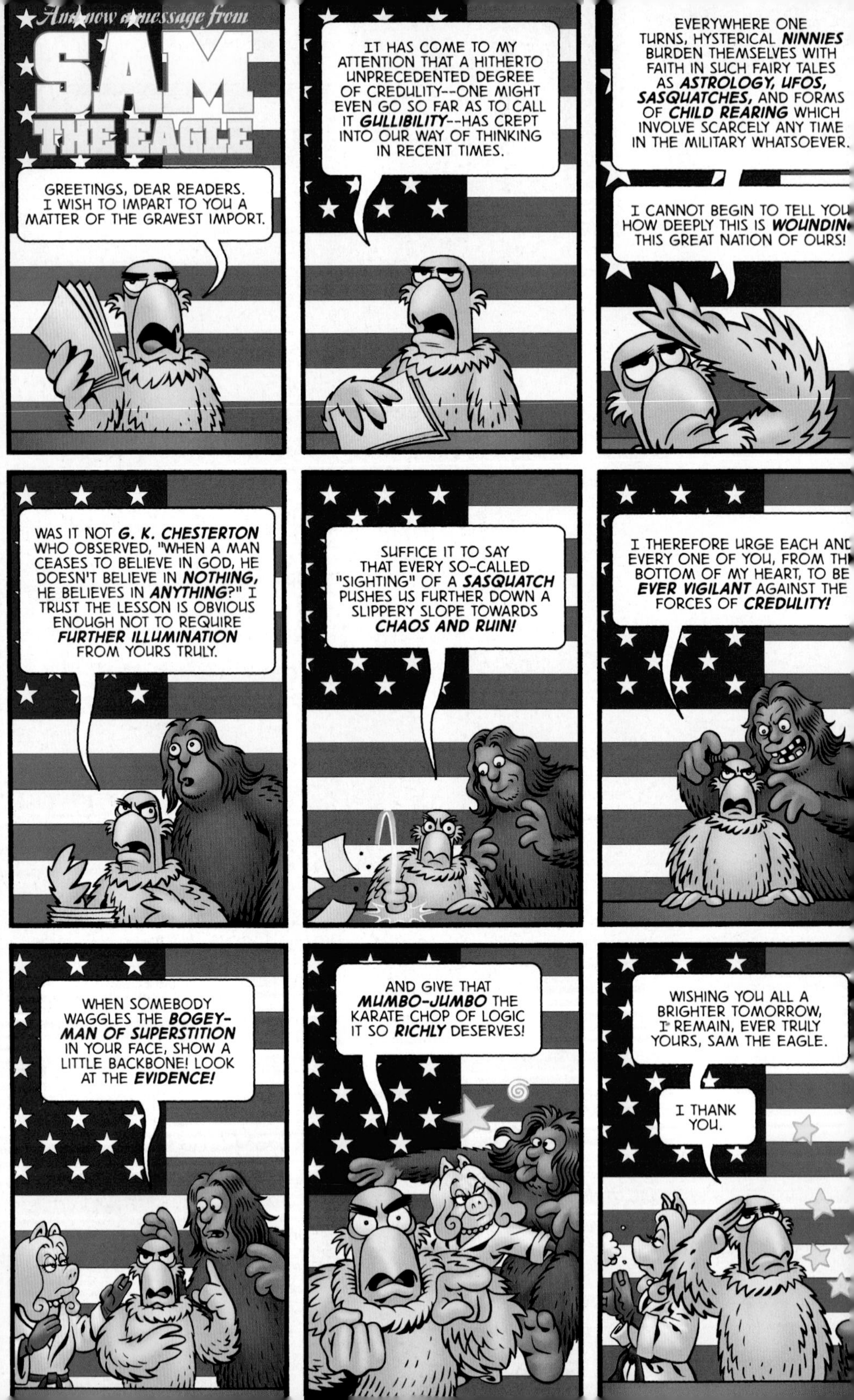
And now a message from
SAM THE EAGLE
GREETINGS, DEAR READERS. I WISH TO IMPART TO YOU A MATTER OF THE GRAVEST IMPORT.
IT HAS COME TO MY ATTENTION THAT A HITHERTO UNPRECEDENTED DEGREE OF CREDULITY--ONE MIGHT EVEN GO SO FAR AS TO CALL IT GULLIBILITY--HAS CREPT INTO OUR WAY OF THINKING IN RECENT TIMES.
EVERYWHERE ONE TURNS, HYSTERICAL NINNIES BURDEN THEMSELVES WITH FAITH IN SUCH FAIRY TALES AS ASTROLOGY, UFOS, SASQUATCHES, AND FORMS OF CHILD REARING WHICH INVOLVE SCARCELY ANY TIME IN THE MILITARY WHATSOEVER.
I CANNOT BEGIN TO TELL YOU HOW DEEPLY THIS IS WOUNDIN THIS GREAT NATION OF OURS!
WAS IT NOT G. K. CHESTERTON WHO OBSERVED, "WHEN A MAN CEASES TO BELIEVE IN GOD, HE DOESN'T BELIEVE IN NOTHING, HE BELIEVES IN ANYTHING?" I TRUST THE LESSON IS OBVIOUS ENOUGH NOT TO REQUIRE FURTHER ILLUMINATION FROM YOURS TRULY.
SUFFICE IT TO SAY THAT EVERY SO-CALLED "SIGHTING" OF A SASQUATCH PUSHES US FURTHER DOWN A SLIPPERY SLOPE TOWARDS CHAOS AND RUIN!
I THEREFORE URGE EACH AND EVERY ONE OF YOU, FROM TH BOTTOM OF MY HEART, TO BE EVER VIGILANT AGAINST THE FORCES OF CREDULITY!
WHEN SOMEBODY WAGGLES THE BOGEY-MAN OF SUPERSTITION IN YOUR FACE, SHOW A LITTLE BACKBONE! LOOK AT THE EVIDENCE!
AND GIVE THAT MUMBO-JUMBO THE KARATE CHOP OF LOGIC IT SO RICHLY DESERVES!
WISHING YOU ALL A BRIGHTER TOMORROW, I REMAIN, EVER TRULY YOURS, SAM THE EAGLE.
I THANK YOU.

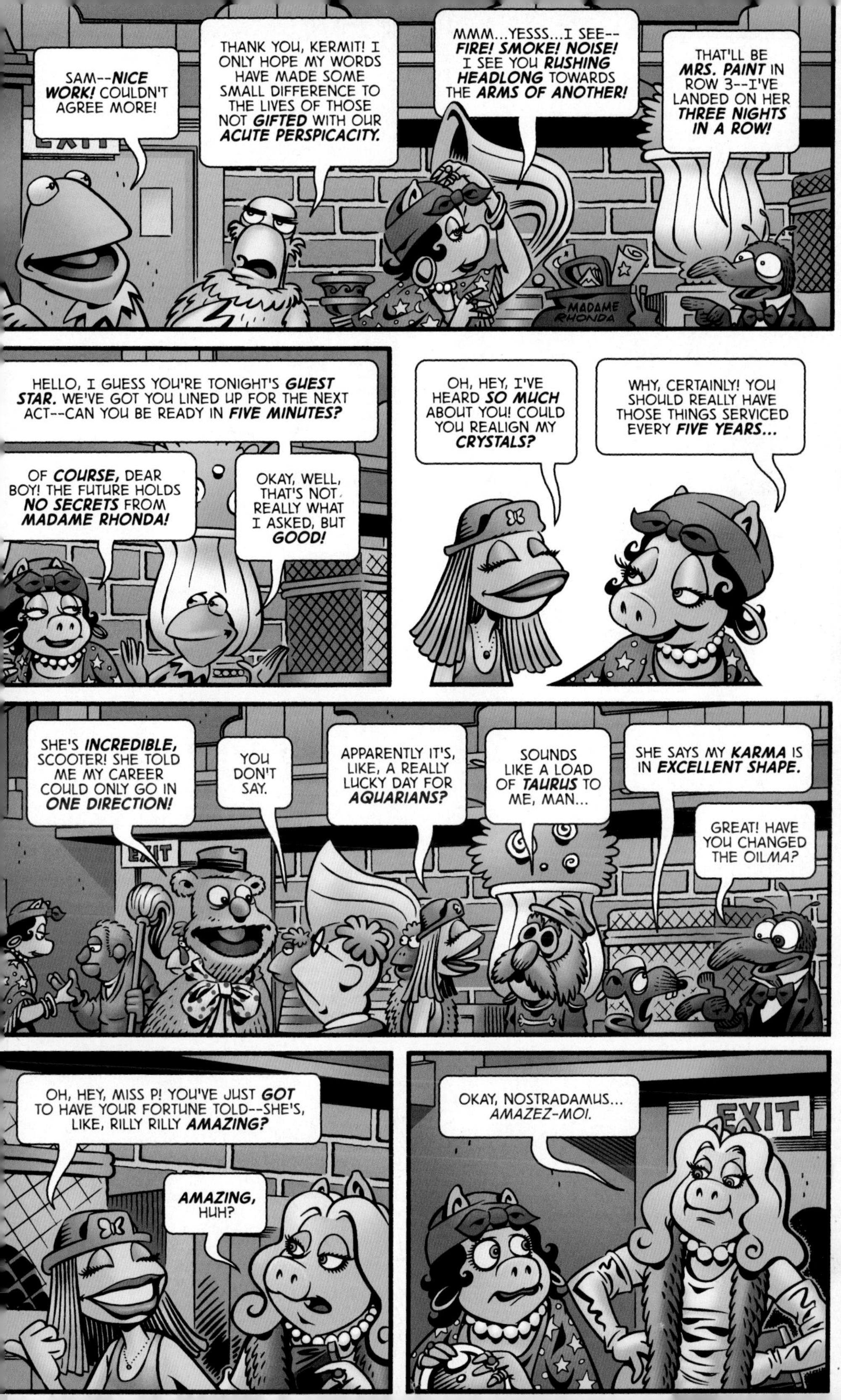
SAM--**NICE WORK!** COULDN'T AGREE MORE!
EXIT
THANK YOU, KERMIT! I ONLY HOPE MY WORDS HAVE MADE SOME SMALL DIFFERENCE TO THE LIVES OF THOSE NOT **GIFTED** WITH OUR **ACUTE PERSPICACITY.**
MMM...YESSS...I SEE-- **FIRE! SMOKE! NOISE!** I SEE YOU **RUSHING HEADLONG** TOWARDS THE **ARMS OF ANOTHER!**
THAT'LL BE **MRS. PAINT** IN ROW 3--I'VE LANDED ON HER **THREE NIGHTS IN A ROW!**
MADAME RHONDA
HELLO, I GUESS YOU'RE TONIGHT'S **GUEST STAR.** WE'VE GOT YOU LINED UP FOR THE NEXT ACT--CAN YOU BE READY IN **FIVE MINUTES?**
OF **COURSE,** DEAR BOY! THE FUTURE HOLDS **NO SECRETS** FROM **MADAME RHONDA!**
OKAY, WELL, THAT'S NOT REALLY WHAT I ASKED, BUT **GOOD!**
OH, HEY, I'VE HEARD **SO MUCH** ABOUT YOU! COULD YOU REALIGN MY **CRYSTALS?**
WHY, CERTAINLY! YOU SHOULD REALLY HAVE THOSE THINGS SERVICED EVERY **FIVE YEARS...**
SHE'S **INCREDIBLE,** SCOOTER! SHE TOLD ME MY CAREER COULD ONLY GO IN **ONE DIRECTION!**
YOU DON'T SAY.
APPARENTLY IT'S, LIKE, A REALLY LUCKY DAY FOR **AQUARIANS?**
SOUNDS LIKE A LOAD OF **TAURUS** TO ME, MAN...
SHE SAYS MY **KARMA** IS IN **EXCELLENT SHAPE.**
GREAT! HAVE YOU CHANGED THE OIL*MA?*
EXIT
OH, HEY, MISS P! YOU'VE JUST **GOT** TO HAVE YOUR FORTUNE TOLD--SHE'S, LIKE, RILLY RILLY **AMAZING?**
AMAZING, HUH?
OKAY, NOSTRADAMUS... *AMAZEZ-MOI.*
EXIT

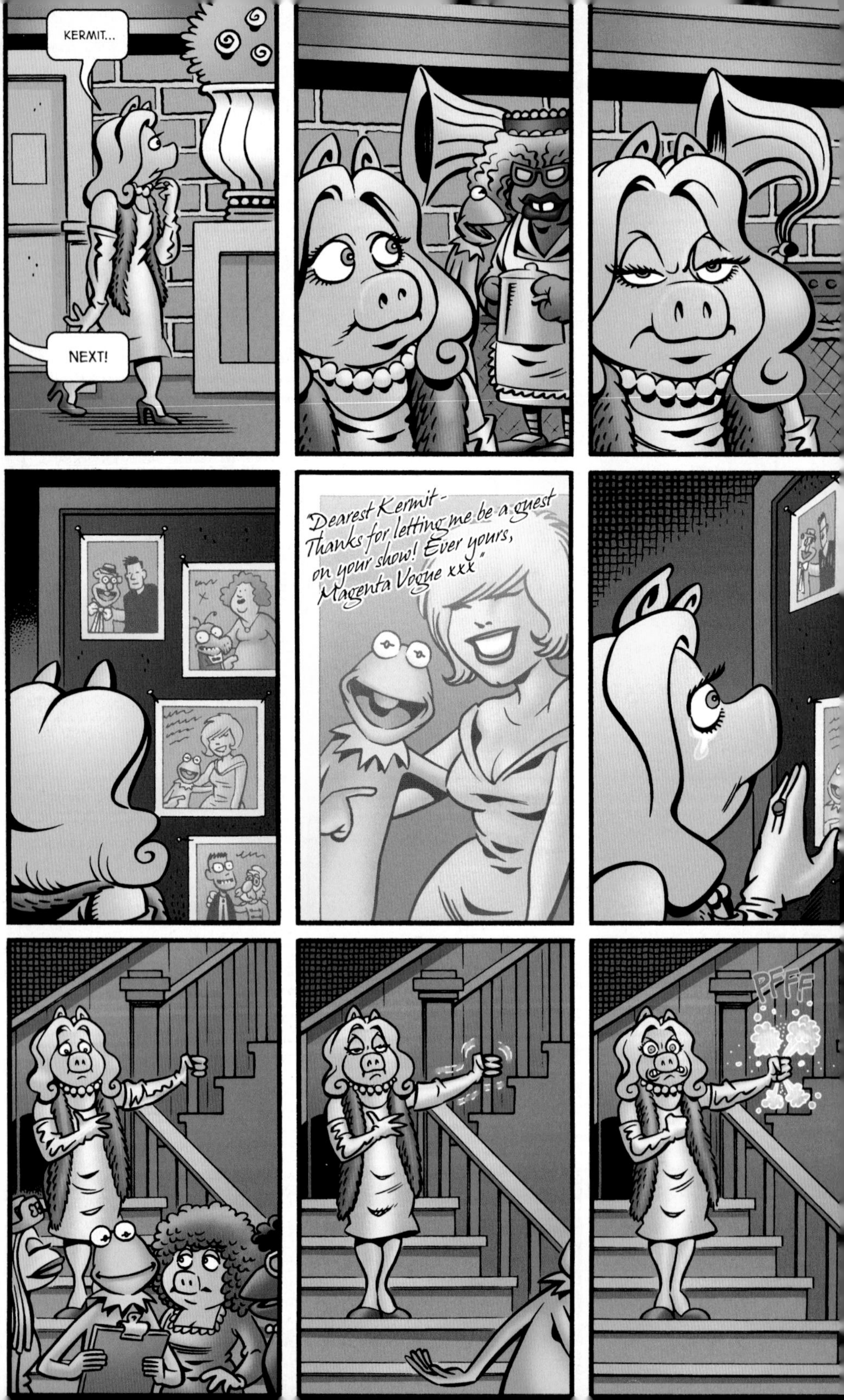
KERMIT...
NEXT!
"Dearest Kermit -
Thanks for letting me be a guest
on your show! Ever yours,
Magenta Vogue xxx"
PFFF

DRUM LINE! *DRUUUM LIINE!*

SHE TOLD ME I'D SPEND THE REST OF MY LIFE IN THE COMPANY OF SOMEBODY I *TRULY LOVE!*

AND WOULD THAT PERSON HAPPEN TO BE... *YOURSELF?*

WORKS FOR ME!

APPARENTLY I'M GOING TO BE REUNITED WITH A *WORK COLLEAGUE* VERY, VERY SOON! *WAHEY!*

SPLAPP

YOU'RE A RATIONAL MAN OF SCIENCE, DOCTOR HONEYDEW. PLEASE TELL ME *YOU* HAVEN'T FALLEN FOR THIS FORTUNE-TELLING BALONEY.

OH, *I* HAVEN'T, MOST CERTAINLY. BUT I DON'T KNOW WHAT SHE SAID TO POOR *BEAKER...*

...EVER SINCE SHE PREDICTED HIS FUTURE, THE POOR BOY HAS HAD THE MOST TERRIBLE FEAR OF *CHIVES.*

MEEP! MEEP MEEP *MEEP!!*

...AND, AS A TAURUS, *FINE CLOTHES* ARE IMPORTANT TO YOU, AND YOU DISLIKE UNPLEASANT SMELLS!

YAR! SWEETUMS LIKE FIIIINE *CLOTHES!*

OH, BROTHER!

FORTY-FIVE...FIFTY... FIFTY-FIVE...

YOU EVER HAD YOUR CARDS READ?

YUP. TURNS OUT I'M A THREE OF DIAMONDS!

AND I WAS A ACE OF CLUB UNTIL THEY CANCELLED M MEMBERSHIP HO HO HO!

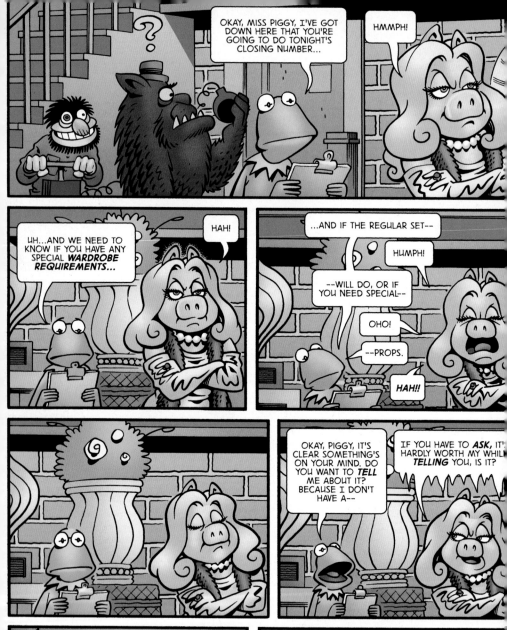

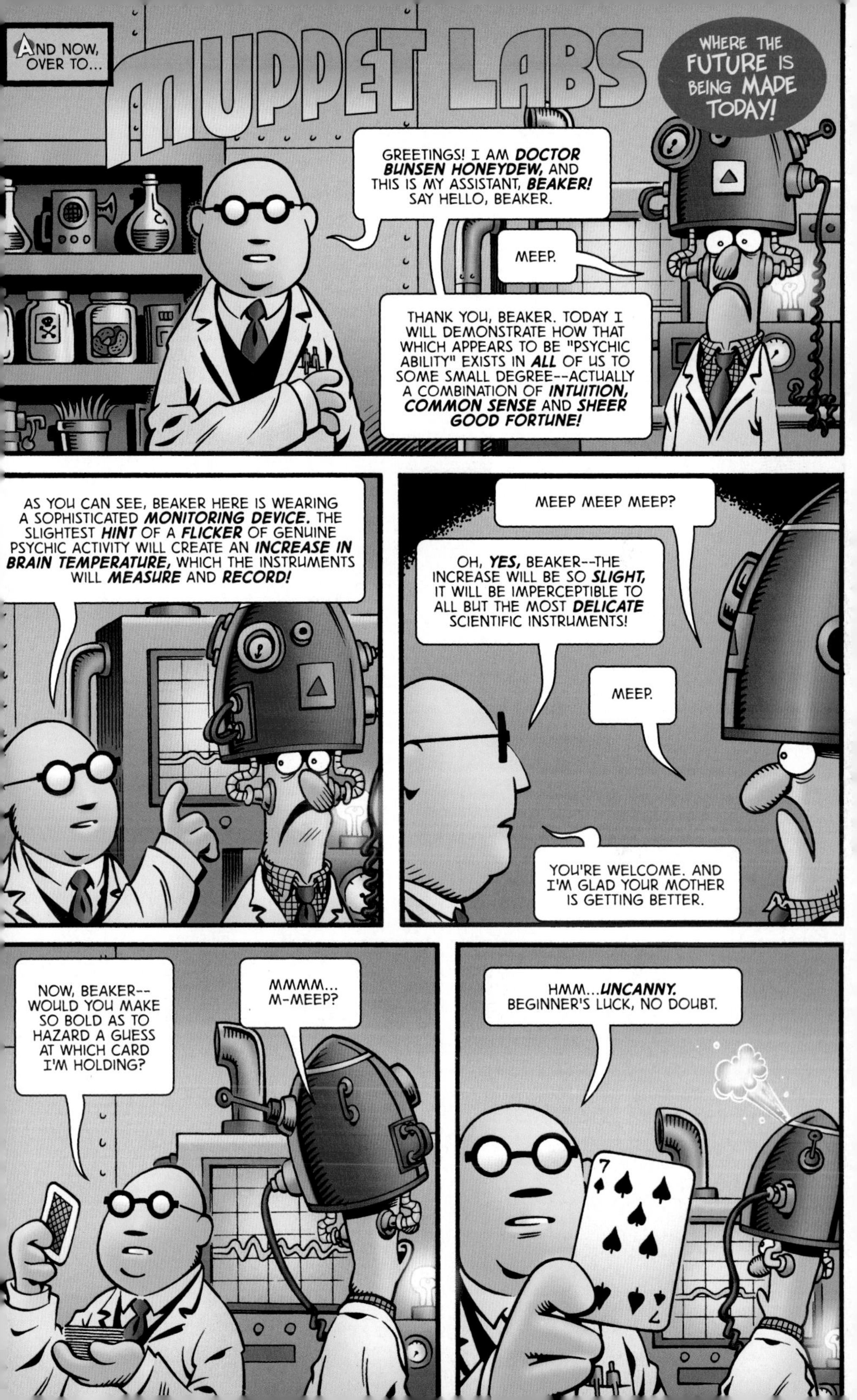
AND NOW, OVER TO...
MUPPET LABS
WHERE THE FUTURE IS BEING MADE TODAY!
GREETINGS! I AM DOCTOR BUNSEN HONEYDEW, AND THIS IS MY ASSISTANT, BEAKER! SAY HELLO, BEAKER.
MEEP.
THANK YOU, BEAKER. TODAY I WILL DEMONSTRATE HOW THAT WHICH APPEARS TO BE "PSYCHIC ABILITY" EXISTS IN ALL OF US TO SOME SMALL DEGREE--ACTUALLY A COMBINATION OF INTUITION, COMMON SENSE AND SHEER GOOD FORTUNE!
AS YOU CAN SEE, BEAKER HERE IS WEARING A SOPHISTICATED MONITORING DEVICE. THE SLIGHTEST HINT OF A FLICKER OF GENUINE PSYCHIC ACTIVITY WILL CREATE AN INCREASE IN BRAIN TEMPERATURE, WHICH THE INSTRUMENTS WILL MEASURE AND RECORD!
MEEP MEEP MEEP?
OH, YES, BEAKER--THE INCREASE WILL BE SO SLIGHT, IT WILL BE IMPERCEPTIBLE TO ALL BUT THE MOST DELICATE SCIENTIFIC INSTRUMENTS!
MEEP.
YOU'RE WELCOME. AND I'M GLAD YOUR MOTHER IS GETTING BETTER.
NOW, BEAKER--WOULD YOU MAKE SO BOLD AS TO HAZARD A GUESS AT WHICH CARD I'M HOLDING?
MMMM... M-MEEP?
HMM...UNCANNY. BEGINNER'S LUCK, NO DOUBT.

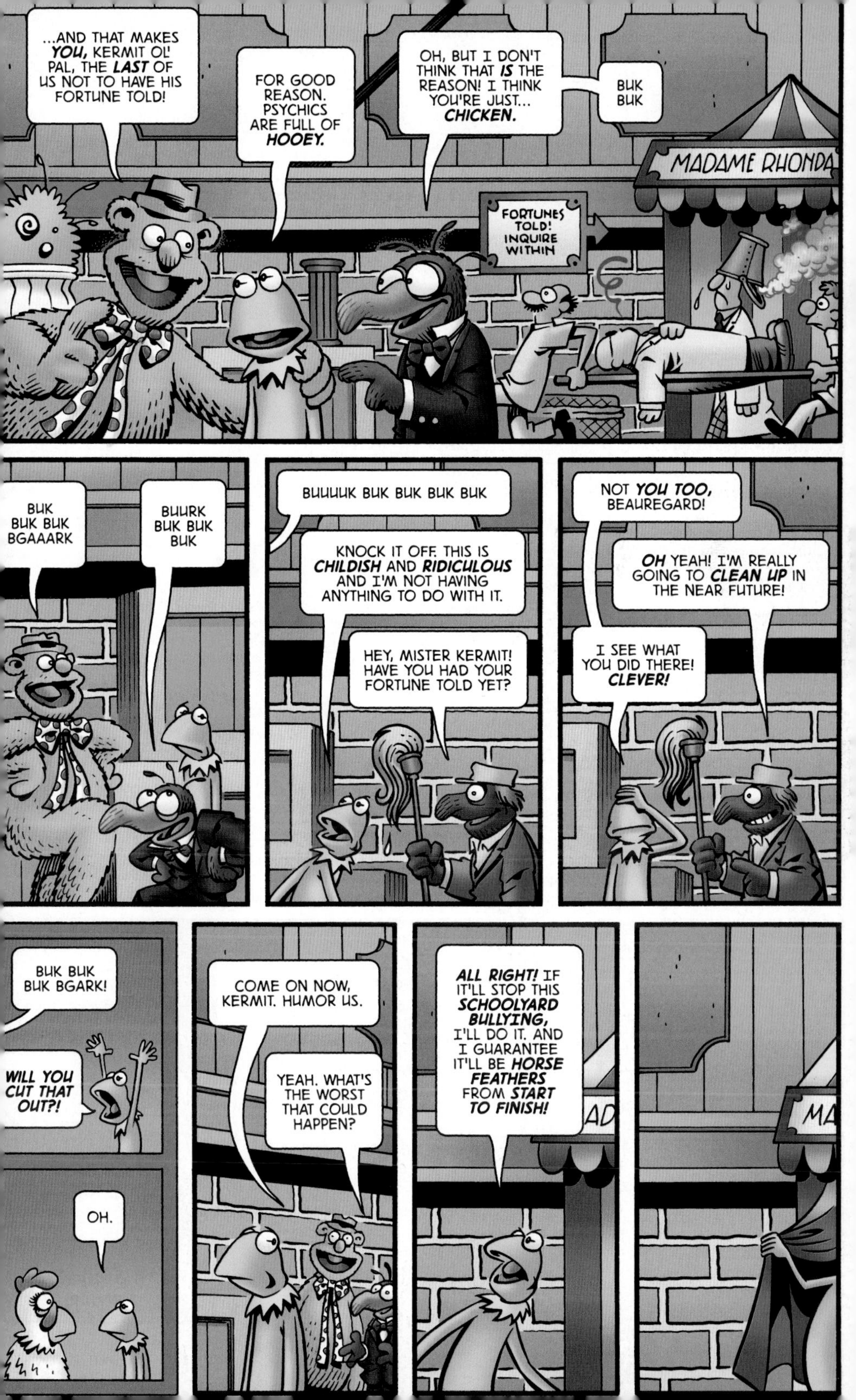

...AND THAT MAKES YOU, KERMIT OL' PAL, THE LAST OF US NOT TO HAVE HIS FORTUNE TOLD!
FOR GOOD REASON. PSYCHICS ARE FULL OF HOOEY.
OH, BUT I DON'T THINK THAT IS THE REASON! I THINK YOU'RE JUST... CHICKEN.
BUK BUK
MADAME RHONDA
FORTUNES TOLD! INQUIRE WITHIN
BUK BUK BUK BGAAARK
BUURK BUK BUK BUK
BUUUUK BUK BUK BUK BUK
KNOCK IT OFF. THIS IS CHILDISH AND RIDICULOUS AND I'M NOT HAVING ANYTHING TO DO WITH IT.
HEY, MISTER KERMIT! HAVE YOU HAD YOUR FORTUNE TOLD YET?
NOT YOU TOO, BEAUREGARD!
OH YEAH! I'M REALLY GOING TO CLEAN UP IN THE NEAR FUTURE!
I SEE WHAT YOU DID THERE! CLEVER!
BUK BUK BUK BGARK!
WILL YOU CUT THAT OUT?!
OH.
COME ON NOW, KERMIT. HUMOR US.
YEAH. WHAT'S THE WORST THAT COULD HAPPEN?
ALL RIGHT! IF IT'LL STOP THIS SCHOOLYARD BULLYING, I'LL DO IT. AND I GUARANTEE IT'LL BE HORSE FEATHERS FROM START TO FINISH!

WHAT? **WHAT?** WHAT JUST HAPPENED THERE?

I'M AFRAID IT'S STARTING ALREADY. *"MUTTON-CHOP--WHISKERED BABOON"*, AM I?

BUT I DIDN'T SAY--

YOU DON'T **HAVE** TO SAY IT! THAT'S WHAT I'VE BEEN TRYING TO **TELL YOU!**

TEN YEARS OF TRAINING AND I END UP BEING ASSIGNED TO **THESE** CHOWDERHEADS!

I KNOW WHAT'S HAPPENING HERE AND I WILL OVERLOOK ANY UNFLATTERING REMARKS FOR THE GOOD OF THE MISSION.

I WILL BREAK EVERY BONE IN YOUR SCRAWNY GIRLISH BODY WHEN ALL THIS IS OVER.

NOW, LET'S KEEP THINGS **PROFESSIONAL!** WE'RE SIMPLY GOING TO HAVE TO **IGNORE** THOSE LITTLE VOICES IN OUR HEADS AND MAKE THE **BEST** OF THINGS UNTIL WE'RE CLEAR OF THE **PSYCHIC ENERGY ZONE!** OKAY?

I AM A BEAUTIFUL, HANDSOME MAN, EVERYBODY LOVES ME AND I WANT MY MOMMY.

THANKS, LINK! WE NEEDED YOUR VOICE OF REASON TO KEEP THINGS IN **PERSPECTIVE!**

I HAVE ALWAYS THOUGHT YOU WERE A POMPOUS TWIT AND YOUR LAST SPEECH HAS DONE NOTHING TO CHANGE MY MIND.

WHY, **THANK YOU,** DOCTOR.

HEY, **BOYS...**

I AM A BEAUTIFUL, HANDSOME MAN, EVERYBODY LOVES ME AND I WANT MY MOMMY.

...AM I IMAGINING THINGS, OR IS THAT SHIP APPROACHING US THE INFAMOUS **SPACE PIRATE, SHIVERS MCTIMBERS?**

I KNOW **EXACTLY** WHAT IT IS, BUT I HAVE TO PHRASE IT AS A QUESTION SO YOU ROCKET JOCKEYS THINK YOU'RE HAVING ALL THE BRIGHT IDEAS YOURSELVES.

OH MY.

IF I THROW THEM MISS PIGGY, I MIGHT YET SAVE MY OWN SKIN!

OH MY.

I WANT MY MOMMY.

OH, BROTHER.

OH, BROTHER.

WILL FIRST MATE PIGGY BE THROWN TO THE PIRATES?

HAS DOCTOR STRANGEPORK GOT REALLY FIRST-RATE HEALTH CARE?

DOES LINK HOGTHROB REALLY WANT HIS MOMMY, OR WILL ANYBODY'S MOMMY DO JUST AS WELL? TUNE IN NEXT WEEK TO THE SUB-ETHER WAVE NETWORK AND CATCH AN EXTRA-DIMENSIONAL REMAKE OF...

PIGS IN SPAAACE!

LATER!

≥SIGH≤ I"M SORRY, SIR. I'LL START FROM THE BEGINNING. **SUBJECT P,** ONE "MISS PIGGY", RETURNED FROM HER DRESSING ROOM TO FIND **SUBJECT F,** "MISTER FROG", SEEMINGLY ABSENT...

...OKAY, OKAY, OFFICER, YOU'RE GOING TO HAVE TO RUN IT BY ME ONE MORE TIME. I'M STILL CONFUSED. WHO DID **WHAT,** EXACTLY?

$100 REWA

POLICE

"NOTICING A STRONG SMELL OF **INCENSE** EMANATING FROM THE TENT OF **SUBJECT R,** "MADAME RHONDA", SUBJECT P PROCEEDED TO INVESTIGATE.

RTUNES OLD! NQUIRE THIN

MADAME

"AT PRECISELY 5:37PM, SUBJECT P DISCOVERED SUBJECT R **HOLDING THE HAND** OF SUBJECT F AND FLEW INTO WHAT I CAN ONLY DESCRIBE AS A **JEALOUS RAGE!"**

SHE WAS ONLY **READING MY PALM!!**

SAVE IT FOR THE JUDGE, FLIPPER...

"AHEM. SUBJECT P THEN PROCEEDED TO INFLICT A **BODILY ASSAULT** UPON THE TWO OTHER SUBJECTS...

HAIIII-YAAH!

"AT THAT POINT, THE FULL EXTENT OF SUBJECT R'S **LARCENOUS ACTIVITIES** BECAME OBVIOUS!"

MY PURSE!!

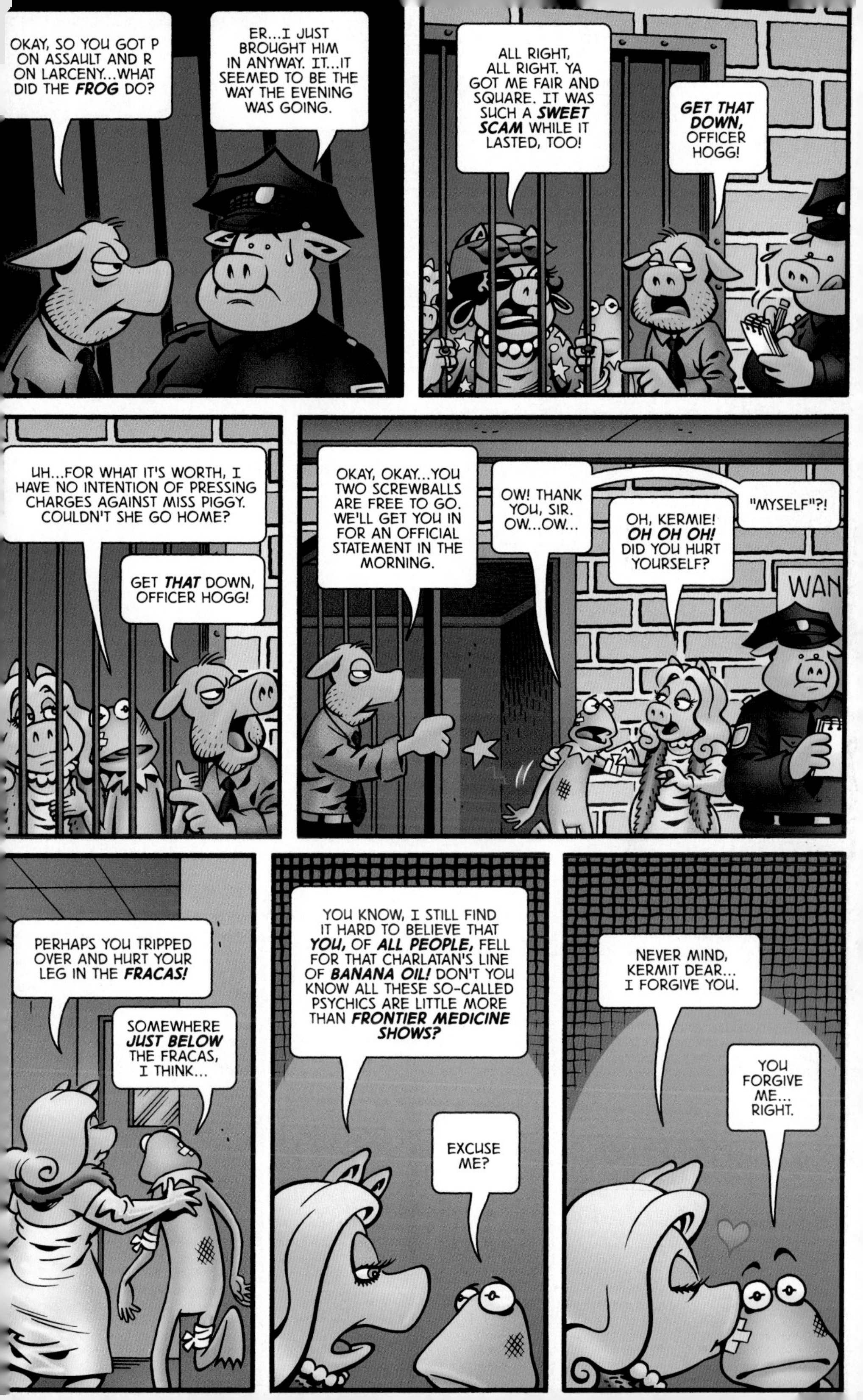
OKAY, SO YOU GOT P ON ASSAULT AND R ON LARCENY...WHAT DID THE FROG DO?
ER...I JUST BROUGHT HIM IN ANYWAY. IT...IT SEEMED TO BE THE WAY THE EVENING WAS GOING.
ALL RIGHT, ALL RIGHT. YA GOT ME FAIR AND SQUARE. IT WAS SUCH A SWEET SCAM WHILE IT LASTED, TOO!
GET THAT DOWN, OFFICER HOGG!
UH...FOR WHAT IT'S WORTH, I HAVE NO INTENTION OF PRESSING CHARGES AGAINST MISS PIGGY. COULDN'T SHE GO HOME?
GET THAT DOWN, OFFICER HOGG!
OKAY, OKAY...YOU TWO SCREWBALLS ARE FREE TO GO. WE'LL GET YOU IN FOR AN OFFICIAL STATEMENT IN THE MORNING.
OW! THANK YOU, SIR. OW...OW...
OH, KERMIE! OH OH OH! DID YOU HURT YOURSELF?
"MYSELF"?!
WAN
PERHAPS YOU TRIPPED OVER AND HURT YOUR LEG IN THE FRACAS!
SOMEWHERE JUST BELOW THE FRACAS, I THINK...
YOU KNOW, I STILL FIND IT HARD TO BELIEVE THAT YOU, OF ALL PEOPLE, FELL FOR THAT CHARLATAN'S LINE OF BANANA OIL! DON'T YOU KNOW ALL THESE SO-CALLED PSYCHICS ARE LITTLE MORE THAN FRONTIER MEDICINE SHOWS?
EXCUSE ME?
NEVER MIND, KERMIT DEAR... I FORGIVE YOU.
YOU FORGIVE ME... RIGHT.

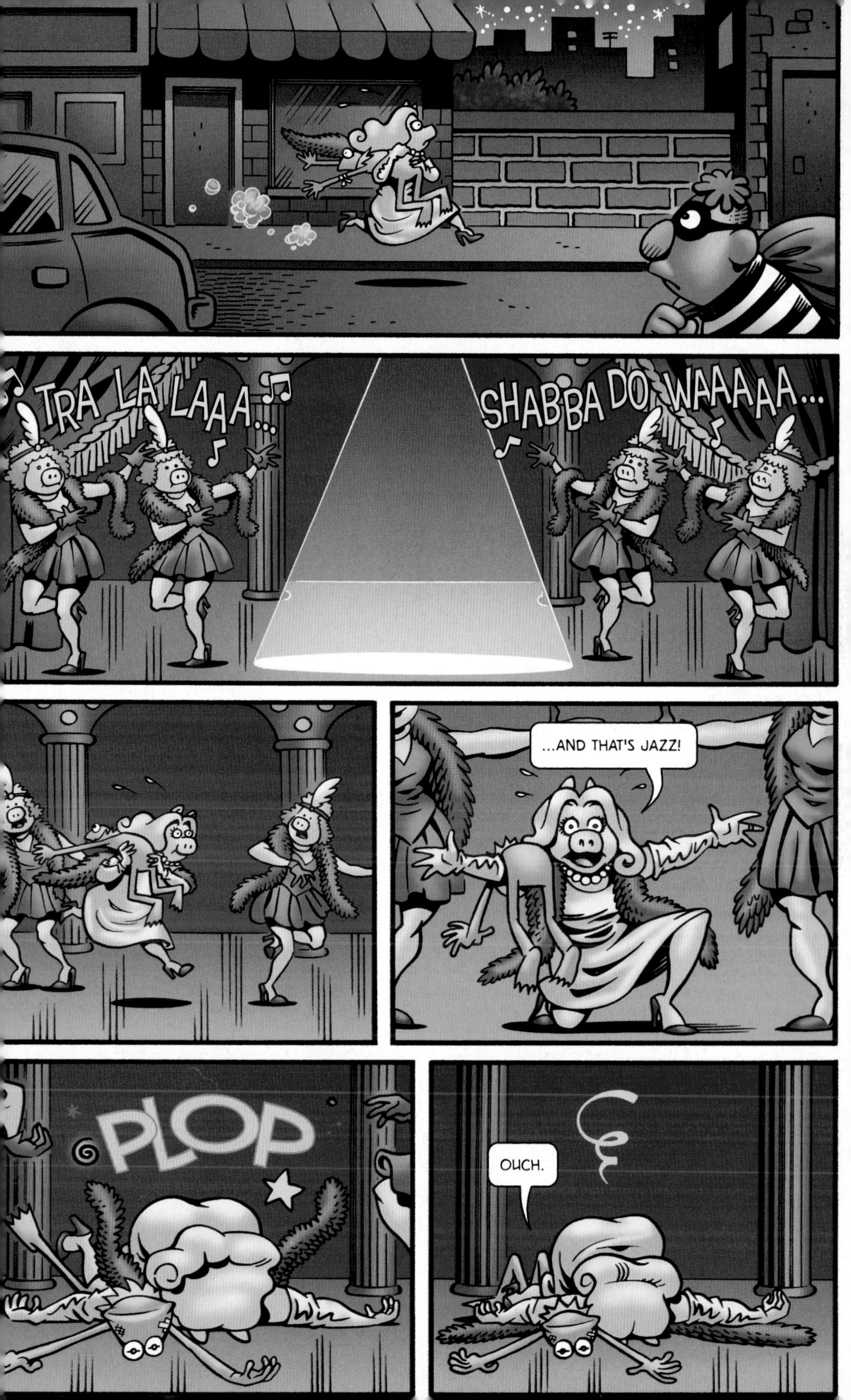
TRA LA LAAA...
SHABBA DO WAAAAA...
...AND THAT'S JAZZ!
PLOP
OUCH.

The En

efore BOOM! Studios approached me to draw *The Muppet Show* comics, I'd already taken a
tab at the characters a couple of years earlier for the magazine *Disney Adventures*. They'd
een running some distinctly off-model Mickey Mouse strips by Glenn McCoy, drawn in a
cratchy, underground-comix sort of style, which had proven popular enough that they were
oking to apply a similar treatment to some other Disney property. I'd been doing a bit of
eelance illustration for the magazine, and the editors at *Disney Adventures* were familiar
ith my other comics work and thought I'd be a good fit for the experiment.

ended up producing a mere 15 pages of material before I got word that *Disney Adventures*
agazine had been canceled. Only one page of that initial run saw print in the pages of
, a Fozzie Bear strip. The rest were consigned to the dark recesses of some hard drive
omewhere, never to see the light of day... I thought.

e thing is, I was inordinately proud of those pages. For the next year, I was aggressively
owing them around to anybody who would look at them, and quite a few people who
obably had no interest in them whatsoever; not with the hopes of finding a publisher or
ything, but simply because I desperately wanted them to be read, by whatever means. And
esumably they were circulating behind the scenes at Disney, too, because BOOM! Studios
entually approached me on the strength of those pages and invited me to do a full-length,
ightly more on-model comic book version of the show.

t me be honest here. The primary impulse for me taking the job on, at least in the
st instance, was to get the *Disney Adventures* pages into print somehow. It seemed to
e that there would be a much greater chance of them finally being published if I were
associate myself with the Muppets for a few months longer and get enough material
gether for a book. Put the *Disney Adventures* in the back as a bonus feature and voilà!
ission accomplished! And the Muppets and I would be done with one another.

hasn't quite worked out that way. The BOOM! Studios Muppet Show comic has picked up
terrible momentum of its own and I hope to be associated with it for a while yet. It's been
e of the most satisfying projects of my professional life, fitting my own interests and
nsibilities like some crazy three-fingered glove. But I'm still thrilled to have my original
uppet Show material presented to the world in its entirety, in full colour and without me
ving to buy anybody a drink, for the very first time. This is the tiny, ugly baby that would
entually grow up to be the eight foot gorilla you hold in your hands today. Enjoy.

ger Langridge
ndon, July 2009

THE MUPPET SHOW

FIFTEEN SECONDS TO CURTAIN! PLACES, EVERYBODY!

FIFTEEN SECONDS?! AND OUR GUEST STAR STILL HASN'T SHOWN UP! THIS IS A **CATASTROPHE!**

KNOCK KNOCK

I'LL GET IT! THAT'S PROBABLY HIM RIGHT NOW!

ALL RIGHT! ALL RIGHT! KEEP CALM... WE'LL JUST START WITH THE OPENING NUMBER...

I MISSED REHEARSALS ALL WEEK~ WHAT **IS** THE OPENING NUMBER?

"THE RODENT DOO-WOP ALL-STARS PERFORM SONGS ABOUT FRUIT"

AT LAST! SOME **CLASS** ON THIS SHOW!

ER... HEY, BOSS...

HMM?

I FOUND **THIS** ON THE DOORSTEP...

GLOP!

NEAT! DOES IT DO TRICKS?

GOOD GRIEF.

HEY, **SWAMPIE!**

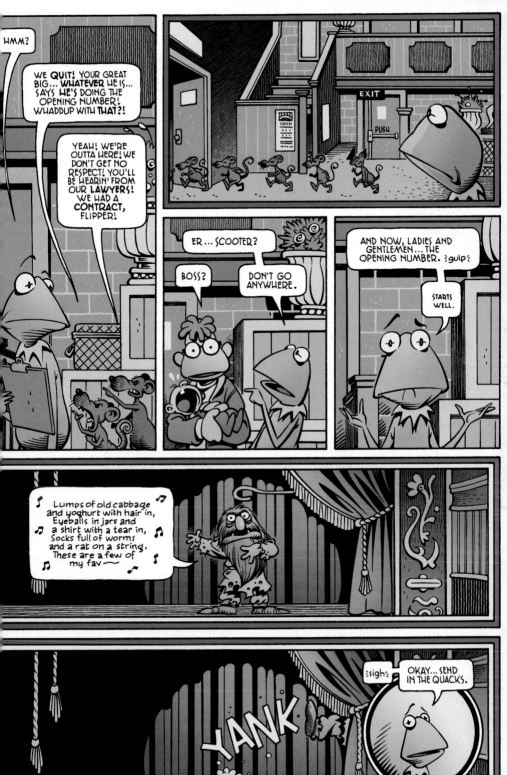

LOCK UP YOUR CHICKENS! IT'S...
The GREAT GONZO!

ARS GRATIA ARTIS

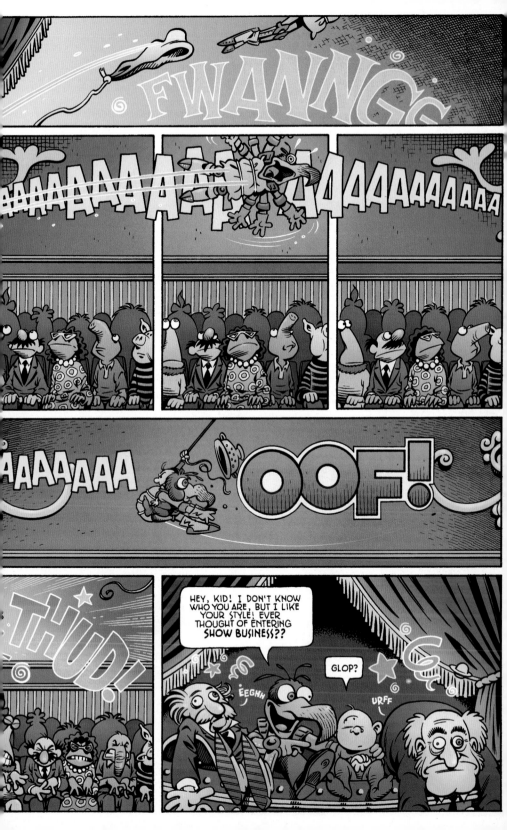

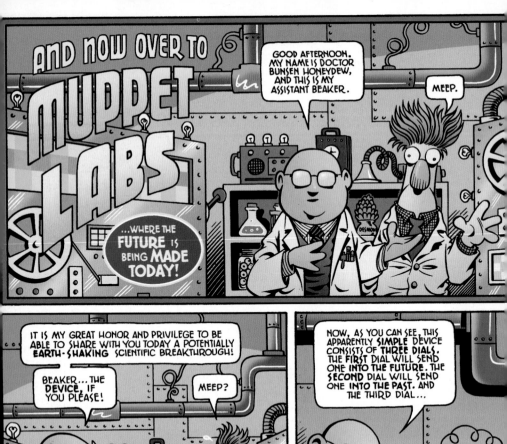

AND NOW OVER TO **MUPPET LABS**
...WHERE THE **FUTURE** IS BEING **MADE** TODAY!

GOOD AFTERNOON. MY NAME IS DOCTOR BUNSEN HONEYDEW, AND THIS IS MY ASSISTANT BEAKER.

MEEP.

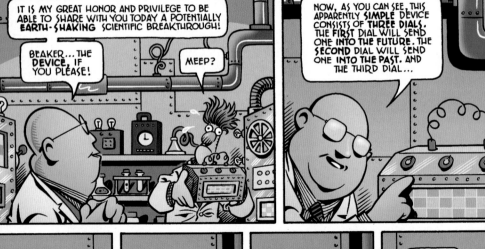

IT IS MY GREAT HONOR AND PRIVILEGE TO BE ABLE TO SHARE WITH YOU TODAY A POTENTIALLY **EARTH-SHAKING** SCIENTIFIC BREAKTHROUGH!

BEAKER... THE **DEVICE**, IF YOU PLEASE!

MEEP?

NOW, AS YOU CAN SEE, THIS APPARENTLY **SIMPLE** DEVICE CONSISTS OF **THREE DIALS**. THE FIRST DIAL WILL SEND ONE INTO THE FUTURE. THE **SECOND** DIAL WILL SEND ONE INTO THE PAST. AND THE THIRD DIAL...

HMM... WHAT IS THE THIRD DIAL FOR?

DING

OH YES. THAT ONE MAKES COFFEE! ≥titter≤

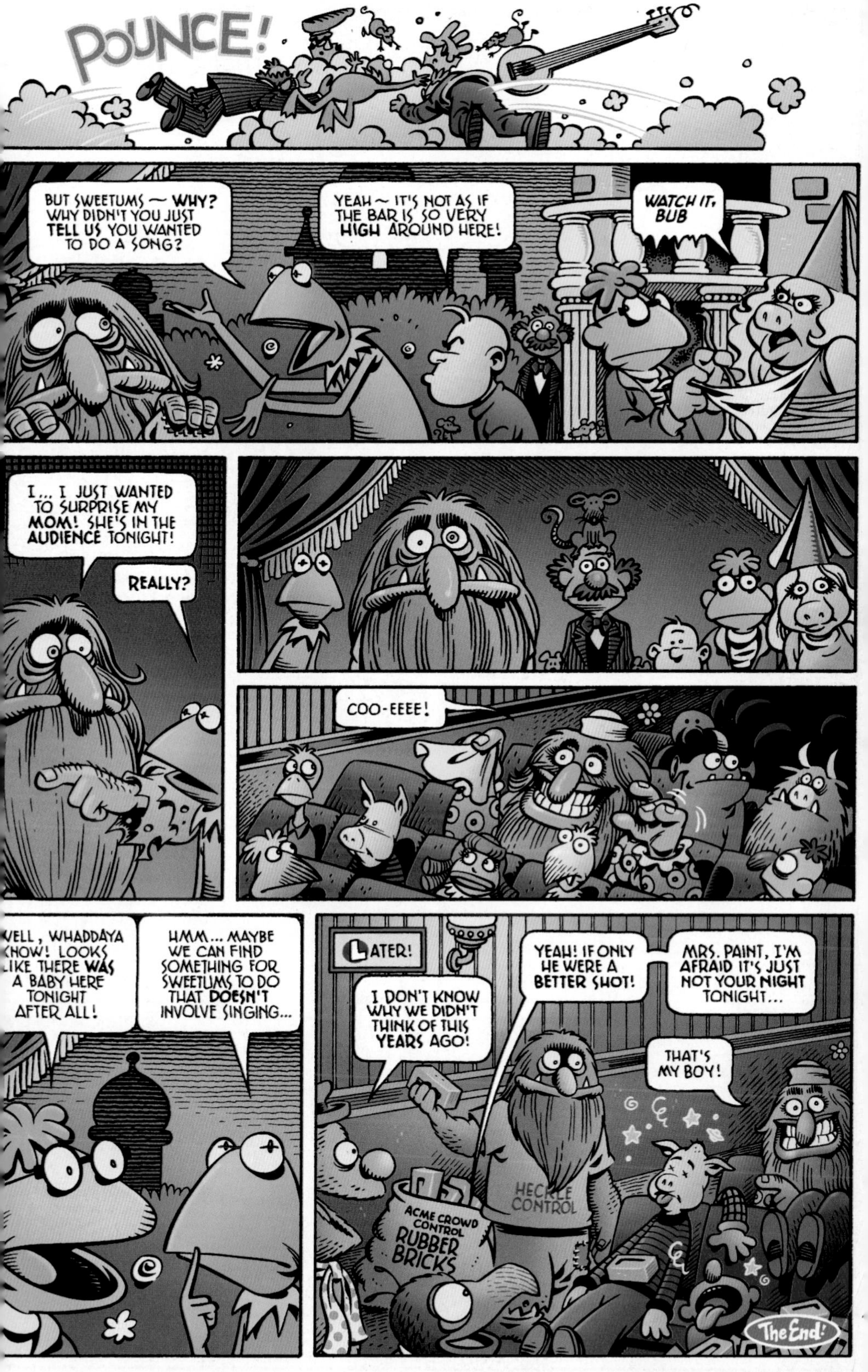
POUNCE!
BUT SWEETUMS ~ WHY? WHY DIDN'T YOU JUST TELL US YOU WANTED TO DO A SONG?
YEAH ~ IT'S NOT AS IF THE BAR IS SO VERY HIGH AROUND HERE!
WATCH IT, BUB
I... I JUST WANTED TO SURPRISE MY MOM! SHE'S IN THE AUDIENCE TONIGHT!
REALLY?
COO-EEEE!
WELL, WHADDAYA KNOW! LOOKS LIKE THERE WAS A BABY HERE TONIGHT AFTER ALL!
HMM... MAYBE WE CAN FIND SOMETHING FOR SWEETUMS TO DO THAT DOESN'T INVOLVE SINGING...
LATER!
I DON'T KNOW WHY WE DIDN'T THINK OF THIS YEARS AGO!
YEAH! IF ONLY HE WERE A BETTER SHOT!
MRS. PAINT, I'M AFRAID IT'S JUST NOT YOUR NIGHT TONIGHT...
THAT'S MY BOY!
HECKLE CONTROL
ACME CROWD CONTROL RUBBER BRICKS
The End!

LADIES and GENTLEMEN! BOYS and GIRLS!

It's that Master of Mirth... That Guru of Gags...

WAKKA WAKKA!

FOZZIE BEAR!

A FUNNY BEAR

A DISMAL PAIR

A TALENT RARE

AN ICY STARE

A SUDDEN FLARE

LIFE'S SO UNFAIR